Essential Amsterdam

by

MICHAEL LEECH

Michael Leech is a travel writer and
contributes regularly to a
number of papers and magazines.
He has written books on
Kenya, Italy and Washington

Produced by AA Publishing

Written by Michael Leech
Peace and Quiet section
by Paul Sterry

Edited, designed and produced
by AA Publishing. Maps ©
The Automobile Association 1994

Distributed in the United Kingdom
by AA Publishing, Fanum House,
Basingstoke, Hampshire,
RG21 2EA.

Revised third edition © 1994
Reprinted June 1995
Reprinted March 1995
Revised second edition 1992
First published 1990

A CIP catalogue record for this book
is available from the British Library.

ISBN 0 7495 0832 9

Published by AA Publishing, which is
a trading name of Automobile
Association Developments Limited,
whose registered office is Fanum
House, Basingstoke, Hampshire,
RG21 2EA.
Registered number 1878835.

Colour separation: L C Repro,
Aldermaston

Printed by: Printers Trento, S.R.L.,
Italy

Front cover picture:
The Keizersgracht at night

This book employs a simple
rating system to help choose
which places to visit:

✓	'top ten'

♦♦♦   do not miss
♦♦   see if you can
♦   worth seeing if you
     have time

INTRODUCTION

The picturesque canals and the houses that line them are a principal part of Amsterdam's attraction to visitors

INTRODUCTION

A thousand years ago Amsterdam was but a fishing village, out on the desolate marshes where two rivers met. The first settlers struggled to keep back the sea (an ever present danger to Holland) and created a dam on the Amstel river. So the name Amstel-Dam was born from that very first sea wall. Modern Amsterdam, large and lively, still has echoes of those early days and it keeps its feet and its feelings very close to water, for, of course, it is a city of canals. Do not be taken in by the banal travel brochure description of Amsterdam as 'the Venice of the North', however, for Amsterdam is anything but Venetian – it is as unique a city as its Belgian neighbour, Bruges, which is often saddled with a similar description. Amsterdam is no more like proud Venice than Venice is like Amsterdam – the city may have been built upon marsh and bog reclaimed from a greedy sea, but there the similarity ends. Amsterdam is uniquely itself, as much a product of trade and commercial aspirations as Venice is, yet quite different. It has an atmosphere and an air that travellers find heady and remarkable. It is a city that one always wants to get back to, however many times one has been there in the past.

First Visits Are Memorable

Amsterdam is a city that extends a welcome, friendly and easy, to the visitor who has been there before, yet it also gives the first-timer a sense of pleasurable discovery allied with that same greeting. People come back surprised at the genial and kindly hospitality of the Dutch, their genuine pleasure in helping strangers and their unusually tolerant attitudes towards others whose tastes may not be their own. Amsterdam is in many ways a 'free city', a kind of San Francisco of Europe perhaps, a place where people can be themselves and do as they wish, and it is an ideal city for the young and those with a youthful attitude to living. It has to be said that Amsterdam is a city where caution must be exercised, however, for toleration of drugs has made it attractive to cult followers and care should be taken when walking or driving in the city. This does not mean it is dangerous – merely that you should use common sense about valuables and

Amsterdam and much of the Netherlands are built on reclaimed land

INTRODUCTION

locking car doors – a camera left in a car, an expensive handbag parked under a chair, can be a temptation in any city.

It is a walking city, so take comfortable, warm clothes and an umbrella, for like most of northern Europe, the city can be damp. Time and the 20th century have changed Amsterdam as much as most places, yet it still retains its character. Unlike its sister city, Rotterdam, which was almost flattened in World War II air-raids and which has risen like a phoenix in modern dress, Amsterdam has been spared for the most part the havoc of war.

You can still find here an elegant city of the 17th and 18th centuries, gilded and glowing with period details, yet as lively and as innovative as ever in its attitudes today. It is a city of surprises, most of them delightful.

Amsterdam Today

The present-day visitor will find a waterborne city of great beauty, with countless picturesque possibilities for photographers. It is crowded, there are many bicycles and pedestrians, bearing home the message that Holland is still the most tightly populated country in Europe and that many of the Dutch have chosen to live in Amsterdam! Despite the pressure of living, most Dutch people will pause to talk and they are particularly fond of their bars and clubs, where you will find them very much at home drinking beer, or Dutch gin, or cups of strong coffee.

Try to talk to local people – you will find them voluble, proud of their homeland, and often very aware of the culture, history and background of Amsterdam in particular. It will give pleasure if you too reveal some knowledge of the city and its history. You are much helped, of course, in that most of Amsterdam's population will have some knowledge of European languages – many being quite fluent in English – and aware also that Dutch is not the easiest of tongues to master. Still, do try to acquire some words, and do not mind if the locals find it amusing at first! It is always gratifying to be able to say 'please' and 'thank you' in the language of your hosts.

Amsterdam began life as a fishing village and has maintained the trade through the centuries

BACKGROUND

After the early beginnings of the village at the junction of the Amstel and the IJ rivers the settlement grew slowly, although it was soon to be recognised as an important focus for trade. Strategically placed, Amsterdam soon began to experiment with other business than mere fishing, and markets started up – before long the little village made itself a free port with special toll concessions, and this new attractiveness for commerce as a gateway from the North Sea to Europe caused growth over the neighbouring marshes and reclaimed land. As you stand on the grand central space before the Royal Palace known as the Dam you can reflect that somewhere under this paved square in the middle of Amsterdam must still lie the original dam. From here the city spread out in all directions, with building fed by the new affluence brought from abroad in a growing fleet of varied ships. Trade created the city; its solid hard-working merchants laid the foundations of its prosperity.

The Arrival of the Canals

A major programme of development began for Amsterdam some four centuries ago when demand for increased docking space and new businesses created the right atmosphere for a new phase, the creation of the canals. They began, as so often with such schemes, in a small way, with the narrow straight canal along the Voorburgwal, close to the Dam, not much more than a moat, but opening the door for shipping to sail right into the city. After this initial success a plan evolved, and the ensuing waterways were created as a series of tightly curved crescents, enclosing the original straight canals. It is a unique plan, and if you look at the map you will see that Amsterdam is constructed on a series of U-shaped roads and canals, one inside the other, and all intended for easy access of shipping. Nowadays Amsterdam's canals may seem no more than sleepy backwaters, disturbed only by the occasional barge or tourist boat, but their origin was completely commercial and if you could waft yourself back a

couple of centuries you would see quite a different Amsterdam, with the canals crowded with shipping and the houses lining the canals all used for the new commerce. With these canals ships could dock right at their destinations and unload safely in the city centre. Look up at the gables of Amsterdam, and you will often

Waterbuses carry visitors peacefully along canals that once bustled with the trading activities of wealthy merchants

see the hoists and supports for cranes sticking out. These are still used today, for the canal houses are tight on interior space and large items of furniture sometimes have to be swung into the houses on ropes and pulleys, through the suitably large windows. These houses were all once storehouses and workshops, upper floors buzzing with activities and merchants living, this time, '*under* the shop'. The canals were limited to four major interior ones (one linked to the river's path out towards the increasingly distant sea) and a girdling one that neatly belts in the old city in its more loosely curved path – the Singel. The River Amstel runs across these canals and is much broader and more impressive as it flows down to the Oude Schans and the docks. Within the old city, and also in the suburbs, are other canals connected to the central system. Most of them will have roads and paths beside them, so they can easily be seen by the pedestrian; although the major ones are cluttered with cars there is a good deal of traffic-free space in the heart of the city.

Foreign Domination
In the 16th century the great empire built up by a conquering Spain, rich on its trade with the Indies, began to crumble. The Spanish had long held the Netherlands and the 'Low Countries', trying forcibly to crush the deeply felt Protestantism of the Dutch and enforcing many indignities on the local population. At last, in 1609, the once powerful Spanish were obliged to make a truce with the rebellious Dutch, and this led slowly yet inevitably to a withdrawal which was effected by 1648. At last, after many struggles and fights for independence, the provinces of the Netherlands were finally free from foreign domination. With a great surge of confidence the newly released provinces embarked on a period of development and expansion now known as the

BACKGROUND

The city has a rich architectural inheritance left by prosperous merchant classes

Golden Age – and Amsterdam was its centre and its spark. A fresh vitality swept through the country, an era of exploration and new trade was launched as far-off countries were drawn into Amsterdam's influence, and concurrent with this came a glorious encouragement of culture and the arts. Museums in Amsterdam and abroad show this new confidence in paintings, sculpture, gold and silver ware, porcelain, fabrics and furnishings, a bursting desire to tap held-down energies and make the new nation splendid in every way. It was a rarity too, for the men and women who were directing those expressions of pride and new strength were not aristocrats but business people who had been brought up on trade. Unlike most other European capitals, where top society was basically one of noble birth, Amsterdam's leaders were of the merchant classes and they brought a new force to this surge of activity, and it is their Amsterdam that we see when exploring the city now – the canal houses, as they are called, in which these merchants lived and worked line the waterways, tightly packed together, a splendid

parade of fine architecture that is very much a Dutch development.

The Twentieth Century

Holland remained neutral during World War I, but in World War II the country was invaded by Germany and during this terrible time many Dutch people were deported, including most of the large Jewish population that had made the city their home. Despite much protest from their neighbours and friends these citizens of Amsterdam were taken to slave labour and concentration camps, never to return. Anne Frank's diary drew the world's attention to the plight of a typical Jewish family during these years, and her house and the famous attic hiding place is much visited (see page 25). Throughout Amsterdam there are monuments to the citizens who went into Nazi Germany to imprisonment and death at this time. Amsterdam, besides being a modern, pragmatic city with liberal attitudes, does not forget the past and the dreadful war years of 1939 to 1945 when many of its citizens faced censure for making public protests about the deportations by the Nazis.

Amsterdam has grown considerably during the past four decades, with suburbs extending across the flat lands around the city to make it a major European conurbation, and it has added amenities and modernised others. Schiphol is a well planned airport, the headquarters of the national

Royal Connections

Amsterdam has always had a royal palace, although it is no longer used as a residence (the Queen now lives in The Hague). Three hundred years ago William of Orange was called over to England, having married James II's daughter in 1677, to reign jointly there as William and Mary from 1689 to 1694. The line ended when there were no heirs, and for the following century Holland alternated between being a monarchy and a republic, eventually gaining its present shape in 1830 when modern Belgium was formed.

airline KLM Royal Dutch Airlines, and it is placed conveniently close to not only Amsterdam but also The Hague and other big centres. (Although Amsterdam is the nation's capital the government meets in The Hague.) There are new connections by road and rail to other European cities, and the capital is well served with motorways (which are toll free).

Trains are particularly well run in this country, and you can get swiftly and easily to all parts of Holland in quicker time than it takes to drive. There is a system of streetcars or trams in the city, easy to operate on zoned tickets which give you a specific time to make your journey and allow for changes, and there is also a new Metro system. Many of the citizens use bicycles and you can rent a bike at the central railway station or at other centres. There are, of course, taxi services too, but with the narrow streets of the old city often much congested you are often better advised to use public transport or to walk. The centre is compact and easy to understand once you have orientated yourself.

Amsterdam is a busy commerce centre still, with a wealth of businesses from cut flowers to diamonds, and tourism is a major earner of money, too. There are many hotels in all categories, numerous places to visit, and good shopping. Holland always has been a leading member of the European Community and has benefited greatly from membership of the Common Market. Most Dutch people are ardently pro European, recognising its advantages while realising that closer relationships with other nations have in no way changed or spoiled a cherished way of life. Residents of this city by the sea are proud of their citizenship, and while at times Amsterdam may seem to be groaning at its seams, with crowds of visitors and business people adding to the stresses, there are always quiet places in this ancient port and principal town where you can look on views unchanged in centuries and smell the ocean on the damp breezes, reminding you that Amsterdam's friend, enemy and ally all in one is never far away.

Amsterdam Today

You can spend many hours in Amsterdam wandering along the canals, admiring the canal houses, monuments of another age – all similar in size and shape and all different, particularly the gables, many of which are elaborately plastered with scrolls and flutings, a kind of exuberant flourish above the suitably sober façades. These houses are now much sought after as residences in the central city, and many are divided into flats. They are strictly controlled by the city, and changes may not be made to the brown brick fronts, nor to the elaborate doorways which are often approached by flights of stone steps. They make a good photograph, especially if reflected in a canal.

The original plan of Amsterdam is much the same today, even with modern accretions and some high-rise building. (Under the streets of Amsterdam are many thousands of log piles driven into the mud to make firm foundations for buildings more than a very few storeys high. It is not surprising, therefore, that the tallest ones in Amsterdam are still church towers.)

The central axis of the city has the main rail station at one end and the Muntplein at the other with the oldest canals running parallel to the line of the Damrak and the Rokin, the two central thoroughfares that effectively cut the old centre in half. To the east of this line is an ancient quarter of old streets with two canals along the Oudezijds Voorburgwal (normally written OZ Voorburghwal) and the

The bicycle is a staple means of transport for the locals, but an efficient tram system also operates in the city

BACKGROUND

Oudezijds Achterburgwal (OZ Achterburgwal. The Kloveniersburgwal with its canal effectively closes this quarter and beyond it to the east along the Jodenbreestraat is the old Jewish quarter and the Artis Zoo. South of the old centre and across the arms of the Amstel river is the Rembrandtplein with its bars and clubs and local restaurants. Next, going clockwise, is the Leidseplein with its lively street life and hotels and across the Singelgracht is the museum area with many of its streets named after Dutch artists. The city continues its sweep from the Leidsestraat along the four central U-shaped canals up to the railway lines along the IJ river with a fascinating old quarter, the Jordaan, slipped in between the Prinsengracht and the Marnixstraat at the northwestern end. Eastwards from these last areas is the central Dam square, with its impressive church and the classical façade of the Royal Palace. Giving onto the Dam is the principal shopping street, the pedestrian-only thoroughfare known as the Kalverstraat. Close by is the famous Red Light District which you can walk through with perfect safety – providing you do not irritate the 'girls'! Near by in the many small streets are numerous bars, often open late at night and catering for a range of tastes, bringing in thousands of Dutch people and foreign visitors every night. Almost everything is available in Amsterdam and the sex-bars are famous, but

Merchants decorated the façades of their houses with elaborate gables and doorways, often using symbols of their name or trade

you are politely warned not to go in if they are likely to offend you. 'Live and let live' is the Amsterdam motto, and it certainly has been good for business! (For addresses and

The People of Amsterdam

People make places and that is as true of Amsterdam as anywhere. The elegance and style of Amsterdam was laid down centuries ago by its proud business people. The fact that this is a city which had to be fought for and defended inclines the Dutch to an impressive passion for liberty and maintaining the rights of the individual. The city is an unusual place, even for Europe where many other cities are characterised by forceful residents – one thinks of the elegant women of Paris, of the style and poise of the Romans, of the solid grey business men of Zürich all contributing to the image of their cities. The conventional idea of a Dutch person is of a straightforward, bluff, easy-going individual of liberal mind – and that's not far off, yet there is a lot more to the Dutch than that, and in a way the residents of Amsterdam can be as different from other Dutchmen as a New Yorker is from a Mid-Westerner. The complex Amsterdam character is reflected in a hundred ways in this waterborne city, yet a few kilometres away in the countryside are communities that surprise with their bigotry and domination by a narrow religious cult. The citizen of Amsterdam has seen a lot of life and, since everything is more than usually 'close up' in this crowded city, he or she tends to be of philosophic bent and quite ready to live and let live. Amsterdam is an unusually 'laid back' city and it also has a very large population of young

recommendations see **Entertainment and Nightlife**, pages 99–104.) The wide windows in which the girls sit with their attractions well displayed are a feature of Amsterdam, yet the industry is carefully controlled and there is no evidence of violence and crime as a rule in the well delineated sex sections.

BACKGROUND

people; in its scattered university and in its appeal to the youth of other nations it has gathered many young people into its confines and their presence adds a note of lightness and freedom to the city.

The 'live and let live' philosophy extends to sex and allows a flourishing of sex shops and allied businesses such as cinemas and exhibitions, bookshops and video-centres. Usually bathed in neon glare or pink suffused lighting, these establishments can be found all over the city and rarely get more than a shrug of the shoulder from resident and visitor alike. The attitude also accounts for the fact that homosexual bars and clubs are common and the city has become a magnet for weekend visitors from Germany, France

Numerous restaurants, bars and clubs make for a lively street life in parts of the city

and the UK to drink and dance in the late-night bars of the old quarter or beside the Leidseplein.

As a stranger, walking in Amsterdam, you often come across an example of welcoming warmth and pleasant smiles, unusual for a big city. The overall impression from shop assistant to bus driver is of an obliging friendliness and interest. People in general seem eager to help, to give you directions, or just to exchange a word of greeting.

On the other hand, Holland is a very densely occupied country with a large number of people filling up the roughly 200 by 100 miles (320km by 160km) country, and at times you do sense an aggressiveness and a need to assert one's 'space'. It is not likely that the short-time visitors will see this side of the Amsterdam character, yet people who have lived for periods of time there tell of

English – Language of the Dutch

Amsterdam must be the only 'foreign' city where English is so universally spoken, with up to 70 per cent of the population having a working knowledge of the language, and where you can get around almost without a word of Dutch. English is a major subject in schools, and the people learn it because it is an international tongue and often necessary for work and leisure. Also Dutch is hard for a foreigner to pronounce with its hard nasal quality and curious twisted sounds that seem to make the tongue do acrobatics in the mouth. This fluency in English is of course somewhat embarrassing to a visitor who has laboriously learned a few words of Dutch, and it also means that in Amsterdam it is hard to practise the local language since most residents will at once obligingly and effortlessly turn to English.

BACKGROUND

Proud householders indulge the national passion for flowers

rudeness and even minor violence towards each other and a need from time to time to show one is not being pushed down by the sheer weight of people.

Many Dutch people have visited other European countries and their knowledge of foreign places and customs can be surprising. The warmth and interest of the people of Amsterdam makes it an ideal first time place for someone who has not travelled much, for assistance is readily forthcoming in shops and on the street. There is a touch of curiosity often expressed too, for Amsterdammers like to know where visitors have come from and what their impressions are of Holland. The Dutch are polite, but they are certainly not shy.

The people of Amsterdam have decided facial and physical

characteristics, being strongly built with big bones and solid bodies. Faces are often bold and even craggy, eyes usually blue or grey and features well-determined. Blond hair predominates, and men will often have moustaches. The young are athletic and well developed, well fed and healthy and they tend to dress fashionably and casually. Children are charming – and beautifully cared for with smart hair styles and modish clothes. Much of the city is geared for children, and family outings to the parks and museums are common, especially at weekends.

The people of Amsterdam are difficult to generalise upon, yet the visitor will find them casual, cultivated and easy-going, and they add immensely to one's enjoyment of their city since they seem to be quite happy that you want to come and share it with them for a time. It is well worthwhile trying to make some friends in this engaging town and organisations do exist for putting people in touch with the Dutch, so if you would like closer links then enquire at the Netherlands Board of Tourism. Drop any natural reserve you may have about talking to strangers, and aim to strike up conversations and discussions – there are numerous cafés and 'brown bars' and even in the trains and the buses people can be quite talkative.

Where They Live

As you come in from the ports by road, or on a train, or by airport bus or taxi, you will pass through extensive suburbs in the way into the centre and this is where the mass of Amsterdammers live in low-rise flats and small houses, neatly framed in lawns and flower beds with water never far away. The suburbs are in general well planned and airy with trees and wide roads, yet there is an overall air of blandness which can be grey and almost grim in winter days when the sky is filled with lowering clouds. Many residents will commute into central Amsterdam to work using the new Metro lines (two of them), buses and bicycles, but rarely cars, for the city is crammed and car parking is very limited. (Illegally parked vehicles are ticketed and often clamped. These areas are marked with warning signs in several languages.)

Cars are ranked very tightly all along the canal sides where there is room, and the occasional plunge into a canal by someone who isn't adept at stopping in time is not unusual! Fortunately the water is not deep and a marooned vehicle is easily dragged out of the mud by a special city crane truck.

In the centre people live on all floors of the houses and a flat in a canal house is highly desirable. It is not a Dutch habit to curtain windows so you will see right into interiors, often veiled simply with net draperies, and particularly at night you will get a feeling of looking into a painting with the beams, decorations and sculpted ceilings of the old houses glimpsed from the pavements below. Windows are very large to capture all the northern light and doors are functional.

Inside entry spaces are narrow and stairs as steep as it is possible to imagine them – all this to take up as small a space as possible and to allow more room for living. This concern with space is evident in all sorts of ways in Amsterdam. Look at the roof-lines of the houses: even they are steeply raked and high and a flat roof is a rarity.

Behind the houses in the centre you may find tiny gardens and courtyards with tubs and trees – almost Japanese in the careful concern with maximum use of limited space. These are usually hard to see from outside, although exploration of little streets and alleys off the main thoroughfares may reward you with glimpses.

An unusual and very pretty formal garden with box-edged parterres and espalier-like trees may be seen off the main Amstelstraat opposite the entrance to Wagenstraat. This is quite a large garden for Amsterdam and is actually part of a museum on the Herengracht (see under **Museum Willet-Holthuysen**, page 29). It dates from the 18th century and is fenced from the busy Amstelstraat with a high iron railed grille.

The Dutch, not surprisingly, are mad for plants and flowers and use every cranny and shelf to put pots on both inside and outside houses, while even in the city centre some houses are draped with ivies and other creepers making whole streets resemble something in the country.

It is well worthwhile taking a stroll along the flower market on the Singel where pot plants and flowers spread across the pavements for a long block, with covered premises behind. (See **Bloemenmaarkt** (Flower Market), page 34.)

Pots of flowers even perch on the many canal boats where people have taken to the water in order to live. Some canals are quite cluttered with boats moored against the sides and some are so constructed that they look more like floating houses than rivercraft. Most of the houseboats will never move, but occasionally you can see one being manoeuvred into a space. Cats and dogs promenade the decks, birdcages hang in windows, laundry dries on makeshift lines and it all looks rather gipsy-like and casual. No doubt there are many problems in living close to the water-line yet these floating homes are neat and comfortable inside, with space most carefully conserved of course, and they can be quite palatial with all amenities and often a wood-burning stove poking its snout of a chimney above the cabin line.

A few people live on the streets of the city but, apart from the drifting 'druggies', street people are not as obvious as in other major cities such as Paris and London where the floating population seems to be getting bigger all the time.

WHAT TO SEE

Introduction

In its relatively small space Amsterdam has many attractions, but one that regularly brings in visitors from all over the world is the array of museums to be found here. Some of the most famous paintings in the world cluster in Amsterdam and other Dutch cities, from Vermeer to Rembrandt, from Rubens to Ruisdael, with a whole modern building devoted to the works of van Gogh. You could spend a week in Amsterdam and not see all its galleries – nor would you be well advised to, since there is such a plenitude of fine things that any reasonable viewer would find it all too much. Take time and plan visits carefully to avoid the fatigue of overstretching yourself: there *is* an enormous amount to see, but there is no point in spoiling a visit with overkill.

The Rijksmuseum, one of the world's greatest art galleries

WHAT TO SEE – INTRODUCTION

Most museums and galleries demand a fee of between 2 and 16 guilders, but if you are planning several museum visits you would be well advised buy a **Museumjaarkart** (Annual Museum Ticket) which for a set price provides you with entry to certain museums for a calendar year (see page 24).

There is a very useful canal boat service that makes stops close to museums. The **Museum Boat** stops near 20 museums, and its schedule is such that if you plan carefully you can go to individual museums, and at the end of each visit the next boat (there is one every half hour) will be waiting to take you onwards. A day ticket costs 15 guilders and includes some other services such as reductions in admission fees at the museums en route, and a guide – though if you know what you want to see you will not find this of much interest as it is only a generalised introduction. A combination ticket including entrance to three museums is also available for 25 guilders. Daily 09.00 to 17.00.

The Golden Age provided the impetus for Dutch art to break into a bloom as glorious as the tulip fields in spring. The new ideas and commercial ventures of the 17th century, when many businesses were born in Amsterdam, created a flow of money and then a demand for beautiful objects to adorn the new houses. In other countries this might have resulted in so many conventional overpainted and gilded depictions of classical, mythical or religious subjects, but while these were occasionally present the individuality of Dutch art of that time is what intrigues and charms, for a new style had been born. In much of Europe at the time a tide of baroque art was sweeping through palaces and churches – still to be seen in Italy, Germany and Spain in a welter of plasterwork and paint – but in the Low Countries there was a different system of patronage. It was not great churchmen and imperious aristocrats who were demanding art; this time it was the newly rich bourgeois and they wanted something different. Pictures and statues were not encouraged in the Protestant churches, so there was no outlet there, but that left the artists free to work for individuals who demanded no set style. Instead of drooping madonnas, flights of angels and sweeps of foliage and feathers set in ostentatious frames or architectural conceits designed for palaces and cathedrals, we get smaller, more compact canvases, suitable for hanging in Amsterdam rooms, their subjects the life of the people who lived and worked in these settings, or still-life pictures, or unostentatious portraits. For the first time in European history, genre paintings came on the scene, and were produced in their thousands. There are many examples of the new and eye-opening works in the major Rijksmuseum, room upon room of them in fact, but you can also see contemporary pictures in more modest places giving you an impression of how they

Van Gogh's **Seascape,** *1888, one of many oils and drawings in the Rijksmuseum Vincent van Gogh*

looked in their 17th-century settings. It is interesting that the trade and industry flourishing in Amsterdam at the time produced so many artists, and some of them world masters whose work continues to be of enormous interest.

Rembrandt's sombre and thoughtful canvases spring to mind, and certainly he is one of Amsterdam's most famous sons with many of his works owing their inspiration to the city and its life. Vermeer of Delft is a mystery man, for there are only a handful of his pictures in existence and these take pride in place in world museums from London's National Gallery to New York's Metropolitan Museum. His detailed paintings of domestic interiors are noted for their purity, their richness of colour and their treatment of daylight tones.

The works of the 17th century supply a clue about the Dutch character today, indicating tastes and values that still remain basic. Perhaps an unsuspected trait is revealed in the renegade artist, Vincent van Gogh, who lived in the second half of the 19th century and belonged to the Post-Impressionists. The Rijksmuseum Vincent van Gogh is a must for anyone interested in the development of modern art, and here you can see hundreds of oils and drawings originally owned by his brother. The 17th century also had an indelible effect on the other arts, and at the Rijksmuseum are

WHAT TO SEE – MUSEUMS

many galleries of silver, porcelain, sculpture, tapestries, ivories, jewellery and furniture – another good reason for making a second or even a third visit, for these galleries are very extensive and present prime examples of works by leading artists and humble craftsmen. Examples can also be seen in such smaller museums as the Museum Willet-Holthuysen (a canal house restored to period opulence) and the Amsterdams Historisch Museum which contains a range of artefacts and objects depicting the city's power and prestige as it grew. In Rembrandthuis you get a strong feeling of what this city house was like when in his early and prosperous years Rembrandt lived here, opposite the wide waters of the Oude Schans.

Modern and contemporary art can be found at the modern Stedelijk Museum (Museum of Modern Art), not far from the Rijksmuseum and the Rijksmuseum Vincent van Gogh. Artists of the last one hundred years, principally, are represented including Chagall,

Picasso, van Gogh, and the French Impressionists. Material also includes sculpture, graphic art, industrial design, posters, pop art, etc.

Museums

◆
ALLARD PIERSON MUSEUM
Oude Turfmarkt 127
Archaeological museum with collection of the University of Amsterdam; Egypt, Asia Minor, Greece and Rome. Small, intimate galleries, are crowded with well displayed pottery,

The city's story as told in the Amsterdams Historisch Museum

metalwork, sculpture, jewellery, fabrics and small dioramas of ancient events in classical Greece. All listings seem to be in Dutch, although there is a brief and not very satisfactory English guide.
Open: Tuesday to Friday 10.00 to 17.00; Saturday, Sunday, public holidays 13.00 to 17.00
Closed: Monday; 1 January, Easter Sunday, 30 April, Ascension Day, Pentecost, 5, 25 and 31 December

♦♦♦
AMSTERDAMS HISTORISCH MUSEUM ✓

Kalverstraat 92
Amsterdam's past in models, sculptures, paintings and photographs set in the former City Orphanage beside the Begijnhof. Part of the museum is outdoors in a beautifully designed arcade with displays and paintings to illustrate the life of Amsterdam's guilds and guards of earlier centuries. The arcade is a public passage (just off the Kalverstraat) and entry is free.
Open: Daily 11.00 to 17.00 (Saturday and Sunday from 11.00)
Closed: 1 January (Museumjaarkaart)

♦
AMSTERDAMS SEX MUSEUM
Damrak 18
This is really an attempt to make the rather lurid sex life of Amsterdam into something 'respectable', but basically it is a place for people to go in and have a laugh. A sort of dig-in-the-ribs gallery showing 18th- and 19th-century pictures and statues and modern attitudes. Probably provides a service for those who don't dare to go into nearby sex shops.
Open: Daily 10.00 to 23.30

♦♦♦
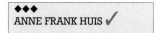
ANNE FRANK HUIS ✓

Prinsengracht 263
The top floor, well hidden, is famous as the cramped World

War II hiding place of the Frank family, who managed to spend many months here in close confinement, their life recorded by the diligent Anne. Her diary was left quite by chance, giving us her vivid views of their 'internal exile'. The experiences and revelations of this young Jewish girl are still moving. In addition there are changing presentations of all forms of racism.

Open: Monday to Saturday 09.00 to 17.00; Sunday, public holidays 10.00 to 17.00. May to September open until 19.00
Closed: 25 December, 1 January, Yom Kippur

◆◆
AVIODÔME
Westelijke Randweg, Schiphol Airport
National Aeonautical Museum Centraal with machines from antique aircraft to space vehicles. Train from Centraal Station.
Open: Daily (except Monday, October to April) 10.00 to 17.00
Closed: 1 January, 4 May, 25 and 31 December

◆
BIJBELS MUSEUM
Herengracht 366
Here there is a chance to see the interiors of two 16th-century canal houses turned into a museum of bibles. Do not be put off – it is a lively and inventive museum with a spectacular façade, and children will enjoy it. The interiors are worth noting for their period details.
Open: Tuesday to Saturday 10.00 to 17.00; Sunday, public holidays 13.00 to 17.00

Closed: Monday, 1 January, 30 April
(Museumjaarkaart)

◆
BOSMUSEUM
Amsterdamse Bos
A forest of deciduous woodland, this 'wood museum' is like a park, but the information centre has exhibits on aspects of this unusual man-made preserve.
Open: Daily 10.00 to 17.00

◆◆
JOODS HISTORISCH MUSEUM
Jonas Daniël Meyerplein 2–4
This is a major museum and will be of interest to anyone with a

mind to learn, Jewish or not. It has been converted from an old synagogue and contains well displayed items ranging from works of Jewish artists to all sorts of objects from home and religious life. Its collection is extensive.
Open: Daily 11.00 to 17.00
Closed: Yom Kippur
(Museumjaarkaart)

◆
KINDERMUSEUM TM JUNIOR
Linnaeusstraat 2
See page 111

A fine collection of holy Jewish objects on display in the Joods Historisch Museum

◆
MADAME TUSSAUD SCENERAMA
Dam 20
See pages 110-11

◆
MUSEUM AMSTELKRING ('OUR LORD IN THE ATTIC')
Oude Zijds Voorburgwal 40
Hidden Catholic church in the attics of canal houses plus furnished part of 17th-century merchant's house. This is very much a surprise museum – tiny, yet fascinating, and the attic church is amazingly elaborate. It really couldn't have been a complete secret when it was built because local people must

WHAT TO SEE – MUSEUMS

The Rijksmuseum houses a vast collection of art and artefacts. Above: stained glass window

have been aware of people entering the house. Musical concerts also feature here.
Open: Monday to Saturday 10.00 to 17.00; Sunday, public holidays 13.00 to 17.00
Closed: 1 January (Museumjaarkaart)

◆
MUSEUM FODOR
Keizersgracht 609
Contemporary work by Dutch artists.
Open: Daily 11.00 to 17.00
Closed: 1 January (Museumjaarkaart)

◆◆
MUSEUM HET REMBRANDTHUIS
Jodenbreestraat 4–6
When Rembrandt was young with many commissions and pupils to teach, he acquired this large house, which dates from 1606, to suit his new-found respectability and income. Later he became impoverished, but at this time of his busy life he was well-off. It is a cheerful house with a view – its gaily coloured shutters and banners proclaim it from a distance. Works on show include 250 etchings.
Open: Monday to Saturday 10.00 to 17.00; Sunday public holidays 13.00 to 17.00

Closed: 1 January
(Museumjaarkaart)

◆
MUSEUM VAN LOON
Keizersgracht 672
This 17th-century canal house,
preserved in its original state,
contains Van Loon family
antiques and portraits.
Open: Sunday 13.00 to 17.00;
Monday 10.00 to 17.00

◆◆
MUSEUM WILLET-HOLTHUYSEN
Herengracht 605
A meticulously furnished canal
house showing the luxurious life
of 17th–18th-century burghers.
The family was wealthy and
socially prominent in 17th-
century Amsterdam and the
house was built in 1687 to show
the riches and possessions of
the family as much as to be lived
in, it seems.
Here you can see wide-ranging
collections of porcelain, antique
pottery, high quality Dutch
furniture and silver, also glass
and carpets and, inevitably,
more pictures!
But the house itself is a perfect
foil, and the rooms are exquisite
with much carved wood and
marble, and painted ceilings
too. It is also very well kept, and
you can see a short slide-
presentation (in Dutch and
English) explaining the
background and origins of the
house.
Note also the charming garden
in formal style, unusually large
for Amsterdam.
Open: Daily 11.00 to 17.00
Closed: 1 January
(Museumjaarkaart)

◆
NEDERLANDS FILMMUSEUM
Vondelpark 3
Exhibition of cameras and
photographic equipment, plus
an extensive library of film
literature.
Open: Daily 13.00 to 19.00 (films
16.00, 19.00 and 21.30)
Closed: 30 April

◆◆◆
NEDERLANDS SCHEEPVAART MUSEUM ✓

Kattenburgerplein 1
The Netherlands Maritime
Museum is contained in the
former armoury of the
Admiralty. There are exhibitions
of the history of Dutch
navigation, and model ships. On
the quay lies a replica of the
East India Company ship,
Amsterdam.
Open: Tuesday to Saturday
10.00 to 17.00; Sunday, public
holidays 12.00 to 17.00
Closed: Monday; 1 January
(Museumjaarkaart)

◆◆◆
RIJKSMUSEUM ✓

Stadhouderskade 42
This vast art collection is one no
visitor to Amsterdam should
miss, even if ideally you should
make several visits (another
reason for acquiring a
Museumjaarkaart for unlimited
entries – see pages 24 and 112).
The building looks a bit like a
palace, although it was always
intended as a museum and has
all the marks of 19th-century
respect for high art – and that

indeed is what you will find once beyond the ornate towers. It is not just a picture gallery, even with its colossal collection. It is the national museum as its name implies and within, in a maze of galleries, are rooms dedicated to the crafts of the country – from dishes to dolls' houses, from silverware to tapestries and a special section tying into the country's colonial past with East India artefacts.

There are three levels to this huge repository; start with a guide book from the desk in the central hall and take time deciding what you want to see. The paintings, in a warren of large high-ceilinged galleries, go from 15th-century to 19th-century works and include famous examples such as the paintings of Vermeer of Delft. This mystery man left very few canvases and these take pride of place in leading world collections – there are several here indicating his uncanny ability to encompass the felicity of calm and repose in colours that seem touched with an unearthly glow – note particularly the blues and the golden-browns. Emotion is suppressed in these canvases and ordinary people going about everyday tasks achieve a quality of timelessness. *The Night Watch* by Rembrandt is a favourite in its own room but there are many other fine examples of Dutch and Flemish art to enjoy.

There is a good café here, but like those in many museums in Holland it is not cheap.

Open: Tuesday to Saturday 10.00 to 17.00; Sunday, public holidays 13.00 to 17.00
Closed: Monday; 1 January
(Museumjaarkaart)

◆◆◆
RIJKSMUSEUM VINCENT VAN GOGH ✓

Paulus Potterstraat 7
A modern museum impressively designed for the pictures of the 19th-century artist, part of the Rijksmuseum. Around 200 paintings and 600 drawings depict his progress and there are also the Japanese prints he worked from. His paintings here include *The Potato Eaters* and *Wheatfield with Crows*. They command such colossal prices on world markets as to seem almost

obscene, especially when they are destined for bank vaults as money-appreciating investments. Vincent lived a lonely and troubled life. After a quarrel with Gauguin he cut off his ear in remorse and was put into an asylum. Shortly after, at the age of 37, he committed suicide, leaving behind a mass of works, many painted in the south of France. The collection includes hundreds of drawings and paintings owned by his devoted brother Theo. You enter the museum and trace the painter's career in a dramatic progress from early experiments to the final fiercely coloured, troubled works.

Wheatfield, *painted by van Gogh in 1888, towards the end of his life*

Open: Monday to Saturday 10.00 to 17.00; Sunday, public holidays 13.00 to 17.00
Closed: 1 January (Museumjaarkaart)

◆
SIX COLLECTIE
Amstel 218
The Six Collection is a private gathering of works of art of the 17th century, taking its name from the Six family whose head was Jan Six. This collector is pictured by Rembrandt, whose friend he was, in a major portrait in this small yet very impressive collection of paintings. (Unfortunately you cannot just wander in off the street – you need to make a special reservation by writing to the Rijksmuseum and requesting a visiting card. You must show your passport.)
Tours: Monday, Wednesday and Friday at 10.00 and 11.00

◆◆
STEDELIJK MUSEUM
Paulus Potterstraat 13
Amsterdam's major collection of modern art from 1850 on, shown in a series of large rooms, in a gallery in the same area as the Rijksmuseum and the Rijksmuseum Vincent van Gogh. Here there is a great choice of Dutch and French art of the last 100 years principally, with examples of Chagall, Picasso, van Gogh, and the French Impressionists predominating, but there are also vast rooms of abstract, surrealist, experimental works. In addition there are often special shows at the Stedelijk as well as film-shows and concerts (quite

WHAT TO SEE – PLACES OF INTEREST

common in Amsterdam's galleries), lectures and theatrical presentations. The collection, which is indeed a huge one, also features photography, posters, prints, graphics, and a range of new works involving many elements. Sculpture too, but then that can be seen everywhere in Amsterdam, and modern design for business and industry is also featured. Early Dutch works are fascinating since they are often little-known outside this country, and these alone can provide an excuse for a long visit. There is a library, restaurant and of course you can buy reproductions of works you enjoy.
Open: Daily 11.00 to 17.00
Closed: 1 January
(Museumjaarkaart)

◆◆◆
STICHTING WERF'T KROMHOUT
Hoogte Kadijk 147
This museum is actually a quay whose original 19th-century shipbuilders' yard has been restored to working condition.
Open: Monday to Friday 10.00 to 16.00
Closed: Saturday, Sunday and public holidays

◆
THEATERMUSEM
Heregracht 168
In a 17th-century canal house, this museum covers the history of Dutch theatre.
Open: Tuesday to Sunday and public holidays 11.00 to 17.00
Closed: Monday; 25 December, 1 January and 30 April
(Museumjaarkaart)

◆◆◆
TROPENMUSEUM ✓
Linnaeusstraat 2
Cultures and lives of people who live in the tropics and sub-tropics are displayed in lifelike settings .
Open: Monday to Friday 10.00 to 17.00; Saturday, Sunday and public holidays 12.00 to 17.00
Closed: 25 and 31 December, 1 January, 30 April, 5 May
(Museumjaarkaart)

◆
ZOÖLOGISCH MUSEUM
Plantage Middelaan 53
Exhibitions about animal life, their evolution, etc. Attached to the Artis Zoo (see page 45). This is perhaps a rather specialist museum, interesting, but the main reason for its existence is as an extension of the zoo's research.
Open: Tuesday to Sunday 09.00 to 17.00
Closed: Monday

Places of Interest
The great array of 17th-century buildings is the main attraction of Amsterdam today, principally in the brick and gabled buildings seen on every side. Amongst them, however, are other unusual buildings and sites, some being unique in Europe – the impressive Dam square on the site of the first settlement raised above the water, the spectacular gilded and coronetted churches rising with stately steeples to make exclamation marks above the red roof-tops, the canals themselves with drooping trees

The Museum Willet-Holthuysen, authentically furnished and a perfect example of a 17th-century patrician canal house

along which the rich merchants built some very expensive and gorgeously furnished houses – some of which can be visited to give an idea of life in such families 300 years ago, the wide waters of the port beyond the Centraal Station, the human associations that reach out and touch a nerve in our own day such as the justly famous house of Anne Frank where the attic hid the family for many months and still tells a tale and, yes, the Red Light District which is often the reason some tourists come to Amsterdam and which still thrives as a centre for the world's oldest profession.

◆◆
AALSMEER
A fascinating visit can be made to the flower auctions that are held in this suburb. You will need to go early to see the loads of flowers arriving on special carts which are taken into auction rooms and sold at great speed using a timing system – large clocks are connected to a computer system which keeps track of sales (you will be baffled to understand how the place works, the pace is so fast).

WHAT TO SEE – PLACES OF INTEREST

The centre is huge yet well organised for visitors – you pay a small entrance fee (children free) and then are conducted along walkways over the auction floors, looking down on massed blooms on the floors beneath.

To visit the flower auction you will need to take a bus to Bloemenveilung Aalsmeer (open Monday to Friday 07.30 to 11.00).

VVV tourist offices can give you the date of the flower parade (*Bloemencorso*) which is usually the first Saturday of September

Flower stalls are an essential part of the Amsterdam scene; this one is part of Singel Bloemenmarkt

and follows a route from the auction centre to Amsterdam and back. The auctions, the biggest in the world and seemingly a sea of blooms, are over by 09.30 so come early to see the action.

◆◆
BEGIJNHOF
Spui

Ancient settlement founded in 1346 by the Begijn Society, this religious foundation has old houses around courts, giving a strong impression of old Amsterdam life. Here you are in a silent part of the city, and can appreciate how this little community lived. Notable are several of the houses, original

buildings in styles of their period. Not to be missed.

◆◆
BLOEMENMARKT
(Flower Market)
Along the Singel, open stalls and boats, a mass of flowers at all seasons (Monday to Saturday 09.00 to 17.00).

◆◆
CENTRAAL STATION
Stationsplein
An imposing, grandiose 19th-century monumental building in the approved palatial style, the Centraal Station was 100 years old in 1989, having been built by the same architect who designed the Rijksmuseum. Ornate, even flamboyant, the themes of its external decoration glorify travel.

◆◆◆
DAM
The heart of the city and always crowded, the Dam is the place to wander around and get the 'feel' of things – from the shoppers crowding towards the walking areas of the main shopping streets to the layabouts. Everything you need is only a few steps from the Dam.

◆
HOLLANDSE SCHOUWBURG
Off Plantage Kerklaan
Now a shell, but a national monument because of its importance in World War II – here the Jews of Amsterdam were herded together before deportation in a building that had played host to Jewish entertainers performing for the local audience. There is a simple yet impressive monument and the site is a park, still stark with memories.

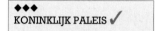

◆◆◆
KONINKLIJK PALEIS ✓

Dam
A must for every visitor to Amsterdam. Although no one lives here now it is an imposing and grandiose pile of masonry and you cannot miss it in its central position at the end of the Dam. It is a palace in name only, having started life as an administrative building, and later being made into a palatial residence by Napoleon Bonaparte for his brother who was declared King of the Netherlands. The next monarch after Napoleon's downfall also occupied the place, and so it continued for a century until the city administration acquired it and restored it in 1935. The interior is fascinating yet stern and heavy, with many marble sculptures and bas-reliefs, as well as vast painted ceilings and much gilded plasterwork. Don't miss the Marble Tribunal, the huge relief map of the city in the early times, or the Civic Hall, which is on the first floor.
The façade of the palace is plain and severe.
Open: daily June to September, Easter and autumn holidays 12.30 to 17.00; most Wednesdays all year.

◆◆
LEIDSEPLEIN
One of the attractions of Amsterdam is the varied street

The Montelbaanstoren, on the Oude Schans canal. The tower was part of the 16th-century defences

life, and you will usually find a great deal to see and listen to just strolling along the streets of Leidseplein.

Here the crowds range around listening to individual musicians, groups, mimes, singers and comedians, all using the street as their pitch and of course hoping for the occasional handout. Some of the talent on offer can be surprisingly good, and almost all are young and hopeful just needing an audience to express their talents and get a round of applause.

The crowds are good-natured and a rapport often builds up between performers and public that makes this casual street entertainment even more appealing.

◆◆
MAGERE BRUG (SKINNY BRIDGE)

The best known bridge on the wide Amstel is the so-called Skinny Bridge, a drawbridge running into Kerkstraat. Once there were many such bridges in the city. Now this is a much-loved landmark.

◆◆
MONTELBAANSTOREN
Beside the Oude Schans canal
A handsome tower, a landmark with its striking double cupola, this is a part of the old defensive system of walls and towers that once protected Amsterdam. It stands in the middle of an old nautical area, and now holds offices that control the water levels in the city's canals.

◆
MOZES EN AÄRONKERK
Waterlooplein
This large and imposing church dates in its present state from the 19th century. It stands in the swirl of the Flea Market and is now a centre for help and a place for locals to meet. Its cavernous interior, beneath the twin towers, houses exhibitions and is a crowded, popular and lively place.

◆◆
MUNTPLEIN
Munt means mint, and one operated here in the early 17th century when the French invaded the Netherlands and the country's mint had to be moved to a safe place: it was transferred here to this little tower, the **Munttoren** (dating from 1490), which formed part of the city's fortifications. This fine round tower, illuminated in summer, makes an exclamation mark and can be seen as you walk down the Rokin from the Dam. The river once ran here. It was moved and the square is now one of the busiest in Amsterdam with lots of traffic and trams. On the island

occupied by the Munttoren are tourist aids and it is also a meeting point for friends.

◆
NATIONAL MONUMENT
Dam
A rather uninspired design, like a spacecraft emerging from a silo under the square, a stone obelisk surmounts a platform on which are grouped several figures representing peace, resistance and the tragedies of war. It is a pity that it is artistically so commonplace for it means a lot to the Dutch, commemorating as it does the many victims of war. It has become a central meeting point. Each year in May a ceremony is held here honouring the war dead – at 20.00 on 8 May there is a two-minute silence, nationally observed.

◆◆
NIEUWE KERK
Dam
'New Church' really means newer than the old one, and this Gothic church is an important centre and coronation church. With its fine, high-arched interior, it reminds you of Dutch paintings of churches in the Golden Age. There is much to see, from intricate carving to the great organ. It is no longer a 'working' church, having no parish, but is used for concerts, exhibitions and state functions. Construction started in the 15th century, but took many years – foundations in the city are always a problem, and many of the houses are based on logs driven deep into the North Sea mud below (so it is not

WHAT TO SEE – PLACES OF INTEREST

surprising that in Amsterdam some of the tallest buildings are still the church towers). The Nieuwe Kerk was the setting of the coronation of Queen Beatrix in 1980.

Open: Daily 11.00 to 17.00 (conditionally)
Closed: January, February Small admission charge for exhibitions.

◆
NIEUWEMARKT AND WAAG

An open space in the east of the city where the *Waag*, or Weigh House, stands. You can pause and sit here, beside the canal, to enjoy the quiet scene. The Waag looks like a medieval castle with its pointed towers among the trees – this is appropriate because it dates from 1488. The square was the setting for demonstrations when the nearby Metro station was being constructed – many old houses were threatened, an old working-class neighbourhood was disrupted, and the Dutch believe in giving voice when they think important things are at stake. Although markets can be found all over the city (see pages 83–4) there is no longer one here, although on Sundays from May to August the Nieuwemarkt is the setting for an antiques fair.

◆
NOORDERKERK

Noordermarkt
This big construction of brick in the form of a Greek cross is still a working Protestant church. The 'Northern Church', if it is open, is worth a look inside – it is unusual and impressive. Built

in 1620, it is a stern, formal building, yet the pews and chairs, now grouped in the middle, give it a comfortable local air. See the vast sounding board over the pulpit.

◆
NORMAAL AMSTERDAMS PEIL (NAP)

Passage Stadhuis//Muziektheater, Amstel
The water levels of this historic town are of great importance. This fascinating geological exhibition shows, among other things, the difference in levels in the North Sea, the IJsselmeer and Amsterdam.

Open: Monday to Friday 08.00 to 18.00 (Saturday from 10.00; Sunday, public holidays from 12.00)
Admission free

◆◆
OLD JEWISH QUARTER

This is a must for anyone with Jewish connections, but it is also a fascinating part of old Amsterdam, even if many of the original buildings are now gone. It stretches east of the city, its main thoroughfare being the Jodenbreestraat, now almost all modern. Synagogues and statues show Jewish historical points and the Hollandse Schouwburg (see page 35) is a national monument. Now a ruin, it was the centre of World War II deportations.

◆◆
OUDE KERK

Oudekerksplein 23
The 'Old Church' stands in a small cobbled square, encircled by charming houses – but it is

*Nieuwe Kerk, on the Dam,
coronation church of Dutch
monarchs since 1814*

also in the middle of the Red
Light District. It is worth a long
visit for its recently restored
ceiling and impressive, beamed
interior. The tower, a delicate
and unusual construction with
much detail and colour, can be
climbed at certain times
Monday to Thursday from June
to September.

Open: Monday to Saturday
11.00 (Sunday 13.30) to 17.00
April to October; Monday to
Saturday 13.00 (Sunday 13.30)
to 15.00 November to March

◆
PORTUGUESE SYNAGOGUE
Mr Visserplein
An imposing building that
managed to escape destruction
at the hands of the Nazis in
World War II. It dates from the
17th century when the Jewish

population was increasing in the city, and by its very size and sumptuous interior indicates the power of the new immigrants. (Jews were given much more opportunity to settle and expand in the Netherlands than elsewhere in Europe, and in Amsterdam they became an important part of city life with banking and insurance interests. Jews were allowed self-government, and in the late 18th century were given civic status.) The synagogue was restored in the 1950s. (Discreet dress and head-covering required.)
Open: Sunday to Friday 10.00 to 16.00 (to 14.00 Friday, November to April)
Closed: Saturday; Sunday (November to April); public holidays and Yom Kippur

◆◆◆
THE RED LIGHT DISTRICT
The liberal attitude of the Amsterdam native towards things sexual is sometimes surprising to the visitor, yet inevitably the tourists flock in to the famous Red Light District to view the goings-on. It is a fairly compact area east of the Dam square in the maze of little alleys and streets along the old canals of the OZ Voorburgwal and the OZ Achterburgwal and around the great rearing tower of the Oude Kerk. Here you will see, seated demurely in pink-lit windows, the famed 'girls' of Amsterdam, sometimes displaying obvious attractions

Amsterdam's Red Light District is world-famous

41

and always clad in the scantiest little bits of lace and satin, occasionally with a side-prop such as a whip or some fetishist object to indicate their 'specialities'. The house may be marked with a red light, or the premises may be little more than a shop window and the 'display areas' are certainly not home – most of the women come in from the suburbs to work a regular shift of eight hours, changing duty, it is said, three times a day so the action is a round-the-clock one. There is a range of women to be looked at – from the exotic Indonesian to the homely round-faced local, from the teenager to the nearly gone-to-seed – it is indeed, a profession where the more experience you have the less money you can expect to get. When someone nets a customer the curtains are closed very rapidly or in some alleys a door is locked, and for a few minutes it is play-time for the hooked-fish, work-time for the woman.

Fair Deal for Women

Amsterdam has had the Red Light District for many centuries, probably as long as it has been a port, and it is controlled by the city with regular check-ups for disease and a register. The women themselves can be quite militant and in this city of toleration and mutual concern even a prostitute has her rights as a citizen. The women have their own organisations and have grouped to pressure the council for a fair deal.

The Red Light District is fairly contained within the central area specified, but in recent years it has also extended towards the Singel and even into one or two of the streets crossing the outer canals, and in the alleys off the Nieuwendijk you will come across sex shops and tattoo parlours, as well as sex cinemas.

Sex is quite a business in Amsterdam, and it certainly encourages tourism. Beside the pink-lit windows you will find the ubiquitous sex shops, peddling magazines, pictures, videos for even the most arcane tastes. Do not look if you are likely to be offended, for photographs and sex-aids, some of them quite bizarre, are on full view in the brightly lit windows.

There are many peep-shows and sex-exhibitions too, and you can wander through them to have a look, even if you don't want to pop a guilder, or a five guilder piece, into a machine in a booth. Again, all tastes seem to be catered for, so don't enter if you are likely to dislike what you see. A complaint even to a police officer would only result in a shrug and probably an unbelieving smile. Few people go into the Red Light District without being fully aware of what's on offer there.

When walking in this part of town keep to the main streets, especially at night, and make sure your wallet or purse is safe – naturally enough this part of town attracts all sorts of characters and at street corners you cannot help but notice the drug addicts.

Gangs of two or three can easily

corner an unwary tourist who has gone into a quiet or dead-end street, and it happens often enough for you to take proper precautions. It is a pity to have to keep repeating the warning, but do take care and exercise obvious precautions when strolling in the city.

This part of Amsterdam is a magnet for gay men, and information on the city can be obtained by telephoning (20) 623 65 65 between 10.00 and 22.00 (also information for women). There are gay cinemas as well as heterosexual ones. Several hotels in the city also offer accommodation to men only. Mixed in with the lurid cinemas and sex-shops are very ordinary and welcoming pubs and cafés, and people live their lives in the flats and houses right in the district. The situation, which may seem an extraordinary paradox to people not used to such straightforwardness, is underlined in the little cobbled square around the impressive Oude Kerk – for here religion faces the oldest profession, and there are even pink windows right up against the church. Lust and devotion exist side by side and seem to manage very well too, but then that is just a part of the unique atmosphere of this surprising city.

◆
RONDE LUTHERSE KERK
Singel, corner of Kattengat
The Lutheran Circular Church, 1668–1671, is no longer a church but part of a hotel, the massive green dome is a central city landmark.

Magere Brug, or 'Skinny Bridge'

◆
SCHREIERSTOREN
Zeedijk, Prins Hendrikkade (corner of Geldersekade)
This tower was part of the city defences and the name means 'tower of tears'. From here wives and sweethearts waved goodbye to departing sailors from the city walls as their ships faded from sight.

◆◆
SINT ANDRIESHOFJE
Egelantiersgracht 105-141, The Jordaan
You will need to look hard for the small door that admits you to these almshouses – *hofje* is a Dutch word which means a small house.
Grouped around the tranquil garden, the houses have black doors with names on them, and neat tiled roofs.

◆
SINT NICOLAASKERK
Prins Hendrikkade
This is the major Roman Catholic church in the city and is associated with a miracle that supposedly occurred in the Middle Ages off the city's central Kalverstraat. A shrine was built on the Heiligeweg, called the Chapel of the Host, to commemorate the event (a dying man, being offered the

host by a priest, could not take it and it was thrown into a fire but refused to burn). The chapel burned in the 15th century and St Nicolaas has taken over the annual celebration. At the time of the November Christmas parade, the church is the finishing point of the procession.
Open: Tuesday to Saturday 11.00 to 16.00, Sunday 10.00 to 13.00
Closed: Monday; Tuesday to Friday mid-October to March

◆
TRIPPENHUIS
Kloveniersburgwal 29
Although this grandly imposing manor house on a canal is no longer open to the public, it did once house the national collection, later to be the Rijksmuseum, in the last century.

Clogs are still worn in country areas but most are now made for tourists and for townspeople to use as decorative plantholders

The house itself, once owned by the fabulously rich Tripp brothers is a 17th-century classical façade, all pilasters and ornamental swags.

◆
UNIVERSITY AREA
The university buildings are to be found around the Spui and the Singel and the area is a gathering place for the young.

◆
VOORBURGWAL
Together with the Achterburgwal this forms the central part of the city – straight canals where the original port was laid out. These old canal

streets are still very beautiful despite being part of the Red Light District, and there are many fine brick houses interspersed with well designed modern houses.

◆

WESTERKERK
Prinsengracht/Westermarket
The crown-topped spire which rises above the small cobbled square by the canal is a city landmark – for decades it was the tallest building in the city. It is still a working church and can be visited. It dates from the early years of the 17th century and Rembrandt is supposedly buried here though no-one knows where. There is a memorial to the painter near the grave of his son, Titus.
Open: May to mid-September Monday to Saturday 10.00 to 16.00. Tower: June to mid-September, Tuesday, Wednesday, Friday and Saturday 14.00 to 17.00

◆◆◆
ZOO (ARTIS) ✓

Plantage Kerklaan 40
The Artis Zoo is an extensive zoological garden and aquarium located in the southeastern section of the city. The zoo is not large, yet the layout gives a sense of spaciousness, and there are many interesting plants and trees – every year in March there is a major flower show in the grounds (*Artis Staat in Bloei*). There is also a very large and comprehensive aquarium, a planetarium which uses a large screen projector

for probing looks at the stars, plus a new geological museum. Beside the zoo (on Plantage Middenlaan) is the **Zoölogisch Museum** with special changing shows of animal life, their evolution and habits. Zoo entry includes ticket for the museum, otherwise a separate fee is made at the Plantage Middenlaan entrance.
The zoo itself was 150 years old in 1988. There is a little farmyard incorporated in the zoo, especially for children, where domestic animals can be seen and tended; there is usually a number of young animals here, too.
On Plantage Middenlaan not far from the zoo are the Botanical Gardens (**Hortus Botanicus Plantage**), with many unusual plants and trees, as well as greenhouses for tropical and exotic items. Small admission charge, café.
Open: Zoo daily 09.00 to 17.00 (*museum* closed Monday; *planetarium* closed Monday until 12.30). *Botanical Gardens* as zoo except closing at 16.00 October to March and open from 11.00 weekends all year

◆

ZUIDERKERK
Zandstraat
Enter the quiet courtyard of this imposing church from a gateway surmounted by skulls and crossbones, gilded bones decorating a 17th-century arch. The church is surrounded by a modern development, a well designed enclave where the only sound is of children playing. The church itself is a handsome one – early 17th-

century and with a gilded spire, part painted in maroon.

No longer used for worship the church features an exhibition tracing the development of Amsterdam from the Middle Ages to the future. You can climb the tower for views of quiet canals in the pleasant neighbourhood.

Open: Monday to Friday 12.30 to 16.30; Thursday also 18.00 to 21.00

Walks
A Walk Along the Canals

You could take any one of the three major 'later canals' constructed in the 17th century (the Herengracht, the Keizersgracht and the Prinsengracht) and see a good deal, and it is easy to swing from one to another given their layout and planning. Any walk in Amsterdam is very flexible and this one particularly so but since the **Herengracht** is undoubtedly the grandest canal and possesses the most impressive houses start with this one, up at its juncture with the harbour, a short walk from the station. Immediately you leave the busy Centraal Station area and start your walk along the waterway you will notice the calm and peace. You could, however, start your stroll a little further back at the Harbour Building (the **Havengebouw**) overlooking the water of the IJsselmeer (IJ) and the modern port of Amsterdam, marked with many developments. There is a restaurant at the top of this building and not far away, if you want to see more of the harbour, is the free ferry

(near the Centraal Station) called the Buiksloterweg Ferry. You will get a better idea of the working of the harbour than from the regular hire boats that cross Het IJ. Walk back into the town from the Prins Hendrikkade and across the Haarlemmerstraat to find the entrance to the Herengracht. This is the smartest of the 'grachts' and in the late 17th century this 'gentleman's canal' was *the* place to live, especially further down towards the Amstel.

Along these canals you will see a procession of gables of all kinds – the official appellations are 'neck', 'spout' or 'clock', and you should be able to spot all three versions quickly

enough. Some of the houses date back to the early years of the blossoming 17th century and while many were the mansions of rich merchants, others have resounding associations – Peter the Great, on his extensive and supposedly anonymous tour of Europe, lived on the Herengracht while in Amsterdam.

Along the parallel Keizersgracht ('Emperors' Canal') you will find a parade of stepped gables, and, at numbers 12 and 16, a fantasy of plumes and urns. Note the fanlights over the entrance doors, such as 111 with

An interesting study can be made of the magnificently decorative canal house gables

garlands. At 123 a redbrick palace (1622) offers a striking façade of the early 17th century, a local monument with busts of classical heroes crowned with grapes, feathers and helmets, the whole swagged with garlands and suggesting well the affluence of new money of the time. The gables continue along the canal in a welter of whipped cream, the plaster in general is well kept up and the buildings are clean. Note that many of them are not actually joined together, and although they all seem to hold each other up at times, you can often see a slice of space between the houses. Later houses have cupids and typical 18th-century motifs. Sometimes you will get a look down a corridor inside one of the houses and a glimpse of an ornate interior, often cluttered with the inevitable parked bicycles! Occasionally you will see an unpainted house, such as at 387 with fruits, garlands, flowers and swags in a soft natural stone.

The little lanes that connect the three canals (the exterior one is the Prinsengracht) are often almost country-like in their appeal – the Molenpad, for example, has trees and creepers hanging from houses (off the Keizersgracht and near the Leidsegracht).

A series of canals cut across the main ones, and you might like to turn and explore the Leidsegracht, a pretty canal paralleling the busy Leidsestraat near by. The noise assails you as you approach this busy street, so continue to detour along the Leidsegracht.

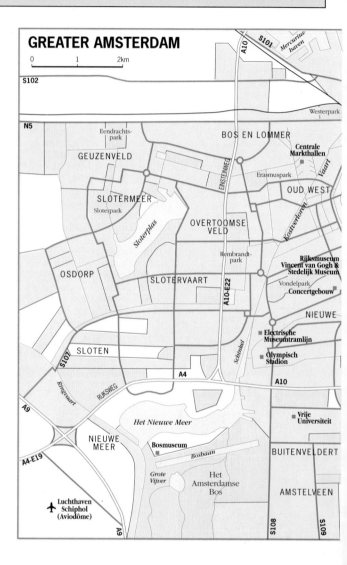

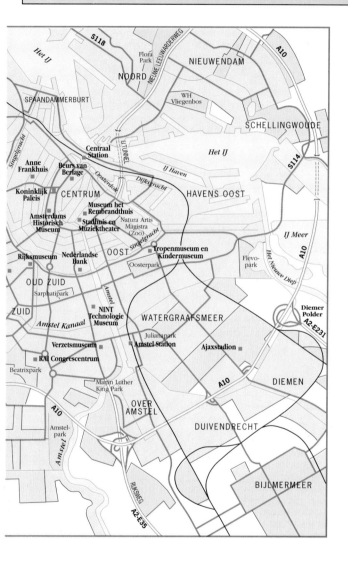

A new policy of keeping the road as narrow as possible on these back canals seems to be in force – some of them have very high, yellow-painted kerbs just wide enough for two regular sized vehicles to pass, and they can hardly go fast along such narrow traffic lanes. Continue to the Prinsengracht and walk on the left along the Vijzelstraat. Where it crosses the Keizersgracht look for number 672, the **Museum Van Loon**, noted as the house of the artist Ferdinand Bol. This is another canal house kept as it once was and, in addition to the family antiques (the Van Loons lived here for many years), there is a series of portraits (open Sundays and Mondays). On the other side of this same canal is the **Museum Fodor** at Keizersgracht 609 (see page 28), a collection constantly changing of the work of Dutch artists. It is an offshoot of the Stedelijk and has special shows in summer, mostly of Amsterdam artists. Return along the Vijzelstraat to the Herengracht and turn right. This part of the canal is replete with large mansions with imposing doors and armorial bearings. The mayor of the city has an official residence at 502, and the Czar's house was 527. You can glimpse something of the social life of the time, however, at the **Willet-Holthuysen Museum** at Herengracht 605. This is real Dutch grandeur of the time, and the big double-fronted house is filled with the most opulent treasures. You cannot miss the beflagged front and the palatial aspect of this canal house, and if you see only one interior, then this really has to be it (see also page 29). Outside is a rare example of a period garden, running over to the Amstelstraat where it is screened by a railed grille from the busy street.

Continue along the Herengracht to its junction with the Amstel (an exotic gable at 568–570 has writhing bird-headed beasts) passing a new development – number 610, a house which now has reflecting mirror in its old window frames. See fine views across the Amstel with the bridges on the opposite shore well lined up for a photograph, and up the river as far as the old Amstel Inter Contintental Hotel. Turn along the Amstel with the **Blauwbrug** (no longer blue, but a stone bridge that apes one in Paris) to your right. A diamond factory, Amstel Diamonds, is on the corner at number 208 Amstel. Go along Amstelstraat to see the garden of the Museum Willet-Holthuysen, cross in to the pedestrian street opposite and take in the view of the new Muziektheater across the water. A short walk along the Amstel will take you to the Muntplein with small shops along the landside – antiques at number 198, a tiny shop with some good glass – and the Holshuysen-Stoeltie diamond factory on the Wagenstraat. As an alternative walk to the right along the Amstel from its junction with the Herengracht and look for the **Six Collectie** (the Six Collection) at 218 Amstel. Here you can find the Rembrandt portrait of Jan Six, along with other Rembrandts and 17th-century masterworks. A small, very choice collection to which you will need an invitation – get one by applying to the Rijksmuseum. Opposite, the Amstel is bridged with its most famous drawbridge, running into the Kerkstraat. This is the **Magere Brug** (Skinny Bridge) a relic of the wooden bridges that once were common throughout Amsterdam and a landmark much loved by Amsterdammers. Walk back along the Kerkstraat, turning right at the Reguliersgracht and go up to the **Rembrandtplein** where there are many cafés surrounding a garden with a sculpture of the painter. This is a

The bright lights of bars, nightclubs and cafés in Rembrandtplein

major centre for nightlife. Opposite is an arcade under a bank building with showcases of modern art. Walk back to the Muntplein along Reguliersbreestraat to find a mixture of shops including Herman Kwekkeboom which sells good pastries, and a marvellous 1920s cinema which is a monument of its time – the **Tuschinski Theater**, named after its creator and an exotic specimen of the period of Art Deco both inside and out.

A Walk Around the Jordaan

This makes a pleasant short exploration of a charming and relatively unvisited quarter of Amsterdam without any major tourist sights save the church beside the Prinsengracht, the Westerkerk. A well-defined area

WHAT TO SEE – WALKS

of narrow slanted streets on the northwest side of the city, it is filled with pleasing little houses and shops both old and new, and has a neighbourly atmosphere and a 'feel' of being a separate town even though it is located conveniently between the Herengracht and the Lijnbaansgracht beyond the city entry road, the Rozengracht. The area is small and notable for the fact that all its streets seem to slant in an almost wilful pattern away from the main 'grachts'. This is explained by the fact that prior to 1600 this was open fields with drainage canals running diagonally to the city walls, and the plan has remained unaltered. (The name is a corruption of the French word 'jardin' or garden). For centuries it was a working-class district and only in the past 40 years after a complete furbishment in the late 1940s has it been a neighbourhood considered worth living in. Start the walk from the Westermarkt, at the **Westerkerk** with its crown-topped spire. A graceful landmark, for a long time this elegant tower was the tallest building in the city. It is still a working church, dating from the early years of the 17th century, and Rembrandt is reputed to be buried here – there is a memorial near the grave of his son, Titus. The gleaming yellow and red crown lifted high over the local canals is a supposed replica of the one presented to the city by Emperor Maximilian in 1489. Concerts can be heard inside

(there is a fine organ) and the interior is worth a visit for its high, spare simplicity. Outside there is a statue of Anne Frank (the house and museum is near by at Prinsengracht 263), In summer the **Anne Frank Huis** can become a very popular spot with long lines of people waiting to get in.

Walk down the Rozengracht until you reach Erste Bloemdwarsstraat, making little humps as it crosses the Jordaan canals. The neat redbrick houses cluster closely, there are unusual stone plaques set in the walls, small shops, creepers growing over old façades. Modern buildings have been well integrated, sometimes complete with jokes as with the large water tap sticking out on the Tuinstraat. At the Egelantiersgracht turn right and walk along the canal to number 107 where a door (the central one) opens to admit you to a tiny garden and a set of early 17th-century almshouses that seem out of this world. This is the **Sint Andrieshofje** (a *hofje* is a small house), once a very necessary social need in an impoverished community. The almshouses have black doors with names on them, and old tile roofs. The Bloemgracht was the better place to live once upon a time, but now the parallel Egelantiersgracht is just as charming – there are ducks and the herons are almost tame as they sit hunched on the banks. Follow it to the Prinsengracht and note the café on the corner – Café 't Smalle, famous for being the original place where Genever gin was first distilled. Across the street is a parade of houses along the Prinsengracht, a variety of styles, often large-shuttered, one with a fake classical front of jokey urns and a balustrade, and extraordinary windows. Cross the leafy Westerstraat and enter the small square by the

The steeple of the Westerkerk, topped by a shining crown and orb

Noorderkerk, a looming construction that is still a working Protestant church. It is worth going in if you can because its design is unusual. Built in 1620, it is a stern, formal building in the unusual shape of a Greek X, yet the pews and chairs in the centre give it a comfortable air. Over the pulpit is an enormous sounding board. Around the church on

Saturday a market unfolds, with a few stalls selling cage-birds. The market extends down the nearby street, very busy on a Saturday morning, very local in flavour. Retrace your steps, or cross to a parallel street (try the Lindengracht) to take you up to the Brouwersgracht. Look for a famous 'brown bar' at this point, Papeneiland, old and atmospheric. In the distance, in the central city, rises the one-time **Ronde Lutherse Kerk**, its massy green dome still a landmark.

A short walk along the Haarlemmerstraat (or the slightly more northerly Haarlemmerdijk) will take you through a busy, crowded neighbourhood with many small shops and cafés and a pleasing, friendly atmosphere towards the centre of town and the Stationsplein. Visit the Jordaan by day or night, but Saturdays and Sundays when there are things going on are best bets, and local people are out walking and shopping with the children in tow.

Excursions from Amsterdam

In Holland nothing is very far from anywhere else and in this small, compact country with its excellent transport system and

Stretcher bearers displaying the round yellow local cheese at Alkmaar cheese market

roads you can go to numerous places of interest for a day or half-a-day's excursion. A trip into typical countryside is easy, if only to see windmills with whirring arms, or the blaze of coloured stripes that the fields become in bulb-flowering time. Coach outings are organised at bulb blossom time (ask the VVV Amsterdam Tourist Office or the Netherlands Board of Tourism in your own country for details), or marked routes assist the independent driver or cyclist. Practically all of Holland's towns are well served by rail, or if you wish to take a guided tour then there are many operating by bus from Amsterdam's Stationsplein or from the Dam, but these will rarely allow time for visits to museums, although good for those with limited time.

◆
ALKMAAR, EDAM, GOUDA

A group of cheese-producing towns which have picturesque markets where the round yellow and red cheeses are piled neatly onto stretchers (check market dates with the VVV). Market days are highly photogenic, and the towns are also old and atmospheric with many brick buildings, mullioned windows and gables. At Alkmaar the cheeses are weighed on large machines, and attendants are often dressed in national costume with women in lace and black dresses and men wearing the typical clogs. Also at Alkmaar, which is the most attractive and therefore most crowded of the cheese-producing towns, there are a cheese and a beer

museum. You will usually be able to view old cheese-making and weighing equipment, and on non-market days these old settlements make charming walks with few tourists.

◆◆◆
DELFT ✓

A very typical Dutch town with a crowded and attractive market and fine brick houses and churches. It is a busy place with many shops and things to see, so plan a day and have lunch here – you can buy wonderful snacks at market stalls, from the ever popular smoked fish to hot sandwiches and pickles. Delft is a walking town of course, with lots of narrow, tree-shaded canals and many opportunities for photographs. There are brick pavements, narrow humped bridges and barges and boats. The churches have the big towers one associates with Dutch churches and the **Nieuwe Kerk** here has an added prominence – it is the

Vermeer

The famous son of Delft is the painter Vermeer – a remarkable and mysterious master of the 17th century whose work is only to be found in major museums such as those in Washington and New York or in London's National Gallery. There are examples in the Amsterdam Rijksmuseum, and a large canvas in The Hague is Vermeer's *View of Delft*.

WHAT TO SEE – EXCURSIONS

Distinctive Delftware: a demonstration of handpainting at a Delft porcelain factory

burial place for members of the Dutch royal family. A fee is charged to go round the church, also to climb the tower for views across the countryside (closed Sundays). The other major church is the **Oude Kerk** and it has a tower with a decided lean! This church was begun in 1240 and within is a parade of monuments – (note the famed Maarten Tromp monument, a battle at sea, all sculpted in marble, also the curiously carved pulpit; open April to October, closed Sunday). Near here is **Het Prinsenhof**, a mansion which started life as a monastery. Now it is a museum of the municipality. (Open Tuesday to Saturday 10.00 to 17.00; Sunday, Monday from June to August, and public

holidays from 13.00). At each end of the central **markt** are imposing buildings, one the Nieuwe Kerk already mentioned and the other the **Stadhuis**, or town hall, while the VVV is between the two. The famous product is, of course, the pottery and you will find it everywhere from market stalls to tourist shops. Watch out for cheap reproductions if you want a good piece, and it is a wise idea to visit the **Museum Lambert van Meerten** at 119 Oude Delft (open Tuesday to Saturday 10.00 to 17.00; Sunday, Monday from June to August, and public holidays from 13.00). Here you will find an enormous showing of Delftware from tea cups to tiles. It is a good introduction to the ware, which when genuine is marked with an imprint. One of the porcelain factories can be visited at 196 Rotterdamseweg.

◆◆◆
HAARLEM

A large town and only a short journey across the flat fields of the westernmost part of Holland to this capital of a province. The town has a spacious and calm central **Grote Markt** surrounded with elegant Renaissance buildings and the great looming shape of the church of **St Bravo**. It is well worth a visit, being a typical large Dutch church with numerous chapels and a famous organ which has been played by Mozart, Handel and other composers.

The painter Frans Hals, best known of Haarlem's sons, is buried here and his works form a magnificent legacy to a town that did not treat him well – he passed his old age in great poverty. (Open Monday to Saturday 10.00 to 16.00; 15.30 September to March.) The pictures can be seen in a museum dedicated to him, the **Frans Hals Museum**, Groot Heiligland 62, housed in a one-time hospice for aged men. His works are stars in foreign collections – his *Laughing Cavalier*, familiar from reproductions, hangs in the Wallace Collection in London. The museum surrounds a charming 17th-century courtyard and there are also works by other artists, with a special wing for modern art. (Open every day from 11.00 to 17.00, from 13.00 on Sundays and holidays).

Also in Haarlem is the oldest museum in Holland, the **Teylers Collection**, Spaarne 16. Here you will find scientific exhibits reflecting the age in which they were collected and made, and the objects cover a diverse range from gemstones to scientific models, equipment and instruments. The overall feeling is indeed of an historic place, for the display cases are all in traditional style. (Open Tuesday to Saturday 10.00 to 17.00; Sundays and public holidays from 13.00.)

A new place in Haarlem is the **Familie Ten Boom Museum** at Barleljorisstraat 19, which parallels Anne Frank's attic in Amsterdam, for here you will find a place where many Jewish refugees hid during the war. The house may not have quite the tragic aspects of Anne's story, but it reveals the bravery of Mrs Corrie ten Boom who later wrote about it in a book, *The Hiding Place*. (Open Tuesday to Saturday 10.00 to 16.30; 11.00 to 15.30 November to March.)

A day should be allocated to Haarlem, for there is much to see in this canal-bordered city. The **Stadhuis** (town hall), Grote Markt, is open weekdays by arrangement, and has origins going back to the medieval era. Near by, the Meat Hall and the Fish Hall, were once covered markets, now are galleries of the **Frans Hals Museum**.

◆
HEEMSTEDE
An interesting little town with many fine houses, an early 17th-century church and the remains of a medieval castle. This was where the Swedish botanist Linnaeus lived from 1735 while

WHAT TO SEE

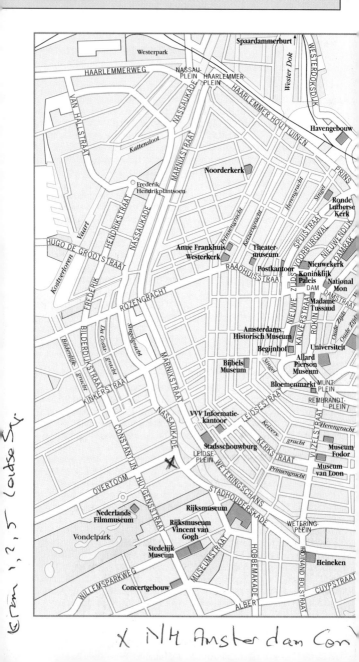

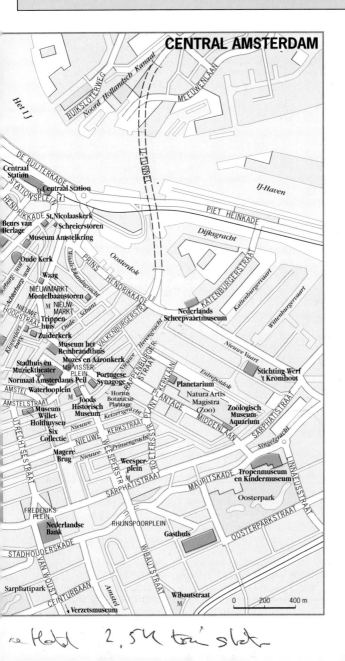

CENTRAL AMSTERDAM

working on the collections of an Amsterdam plant enthusiast. The **Museum De Cruquius** has a restored steam pump (open every day).

◆
HOORN
In the north of the country (the town which gave its name to Cape Horn), this place has a beguiling country-town charm.

KEUKENHOF
See **Lisse**, below.

◆
LEIDEN
This is the seat of Holland's most ancient university, and the town is handsome and not only possesses museums bit also has associations with the Pilgrim Fathers on their peregrinations around Europe in search of tolerance for their beliefs. There is a **Pilgrim Fathers Documents Centre** at Vliet 45 (open Monday to Friday 09.30 to 16.30), and John Robinson, one of the guiding lights of the group, is buried at the vast brick **Sint Pieterkerk** in the centre of the town.

The centre of Leiden is handsome and well preserved. For 400 years the university's buildings have been along the Rapenburg with the **Academie** reflected in the canal, the main centre. The VVV Tourist Office is on the Stationsplein, and you can take boat rides on the waterways. The museums include the **Rijksmuseum van Oudheden** (National Museum of Antiquities) at Rapenburg 28 (open Tuesday to Saturday 10.00 to 17.00; Sunday and public holidays from 12.00), and the **Lakenhal**, Oude Singel 28-32, which is now the municipal museum but was once the guildhall of the clothmakers (open Friday 10.00 to 17.00; Saturday, Sunday and public holidays from 12.00). Here you will find paintings (Rembrandt was from Leiden) and local crafts. The **Rijksmuseum voor Volkenkunde,** 1 Steenstraat, covers the subject of ethnology (open Tuesday to Friday 10.00 to 17.00; Saturday, Sunday and public holidays from 12.00).

◆◆
LISSE
In this town near Haarlem you will find the famous Gardens of **Keukenhof**. Here, in spring, there is a host of flowering bulbs. The setting is ravishing with wooded dells and grassy spaces. This is in the middle of the tulip area and so is very popular for tourists in spring (open late March to late May only, daily 08.00 to 20.00 – last admission 18.30). Near by are extensive sand dunes.

◆
MIDDELBURG
A good distance from Amsterdam, but if you wish to see people in national costume worn as an everyday dress, it is one of the places to visit. Here you will find a small, redbrick town in the middle of the wide flat marshland of the south.

◆
ROTTERDAM
A modern city, almost totally destroyed in the last war, Rotterdam has risen again in a

striking modern design and is now the centre of the world's busiest seaport, **Europoort**. It has much to offer, even if all its ancient houses and most of its historical associations are now memories. There is a gallery of major importance, the **Museum Boymans van Beuningen**; Flemish and Dutch masters and a modern collection make this a place to note. (Open Tuesday to Saturday 10.00 to 17.00; Sunday and public holidays from 11.00.) A part of the town that has been preserved in its ancient style is **Delfshaven** the quarter from which the Pilgrim Fathers departed in 1620. The birthplace of Erasmus, Rotterdam offers city and port tours. Check at the VVV Tourist Office at the Centraal Station, or by the Stadhuis.

◆◆
THE HAGUE
Plan a whole day here: there is lots to see and do. It is the centre of government and is close to the sea with a beach at **Scheveningen**. The main attraction here is the **Binnenhof**, (open Monday to Saturday 10.00

Tulips near Amsterdam – literally millions of them, at the Keukenhof in Lisse

to 16.00; from 12.00 July and August). The inner court of the castle of the Counts of Holland standing on the Hof Vijver ornamental lake. It is now the home of the Dutch government and the two chambers meet in the 13th-century **Ridderzaal** (Knight's Hall) which can be visited, when not in use, on a conducted tour.

The hall is the setting of the state opening of Parliament. William V's collection can be seen at the **Schilderijengalerij Prins Willem V** (open Tuesday to Sunday 11.00 to 16.00 early April to December) and is a typical 17th-century picture collection. It stands in the **Buitenhof**, the old outer court of the original castle.

Near by is the old Prison Gate, **Gevangenpoort**, with a collection of torture instruments (open Monday to Friday 10.00 to 17.00; Sunday from 13.00. In the Binnenhof court is a small museum that should not be missed on any account – the **Mauritshuis** has a very fine collection of paintings of Holland's great age; this Royal Picture Gallery is housed in a renovated Renaissance palace. (Open Tuesday to Saturday 10.00 to 17.00; Sunday and public holidays from 11.00.) Also in The Hague is the **Oude Stadhuis** of the 16th century, the **Grote Kerk**, several other notable museums and a curiosity, the **Panorama Mesdag** with a huge circular painting of 19th-century Scheveningen.

The **Paleis Noordeinde** is the official home of the monarch, and also in the suburbs is **Madurodam**, the model city (see page 111).

◆
VOLENDAM, MONNICKENDAM, MARKEN
Although a popular choice for the numerous coach companies operating out of Amsterdam, **Volendam** is a much overrated town even though it does give the chance to see fishermen wearing baggy black pants and clogs and women in starched lace. Pop in and take a short visit – there are only a couple of spots to look for and along the quay you will see the boats and the tackle, and the rather self-conscious residents. Not for the discriminating – perhaps you would be better off trying **Monnickendam** which is close by and less visited yet has a decided atmosphere and a charm of its own. Both these places are a short distance from Amsterdam and can easily be visited in half a day (many tours are on offer around the Stationsplein in Amsterdam). **Marken** is another very popular spot, but despite its crowded aspect it still has an intriguing air due to its isolated position on what was once the North Sea. The houses are painted and raised on piles or mounds.

◆
ZANDVOORT
A beach resort near Haarlem which offers good sand and shallow sloping beaches with dunes in the background. There is a national dune park here, **Kennemerduinen**, for nature lovers, and the bulb fields stretch away to the south.

PEACE AND QUIET

Wildlife and Countryside in and around Amsterdam
by Paul Sterry

The Netherlands is one of the lowest-lying countries in Europe, with much of the land lying at or below sea level and, despite this rather precarious existence, it is also one of the most densely populated regions. Much of the remaining land which is not built on is devoted to farming, and this land-use comprises nearly half the total land area. Fortunately, much of the agriculture is not as intense as in other areas of Europe and many of the farming practices and methods actually benefit elements of the wildlife. In particular, breeding wading birds such as the black-tailed godwit reach very high densities in the grazing pastures around Amsterdam. This elegant bird is just one of the 150 species which regularly breed in Dutch pastures, dunes, woodlands and wetlands.

The Netherlands has an extensive coastline with both young and stabilised sand dunes. The proximity of the sea as well as the pastures and wetlands, make this city an ideal base from which to explore the wildlife.

For peace and quiet in Amsterdam visit the Botanical Gardens (Hortus Botanicus Plantage) on Plantage Middenlaan (open daily), Ooster Park on Oosterparkstraat and Vondel Park on Consantijn

A black-tailed godwit. The beak of this wader is packed with sensory cells which enable it to track its prey in deep mud

PEACE AND QUIET

Huygensstraat. Ponds and lakes in the latter two sites attract black-headed gulls, mallards and coots. During the winter months, waterbirds and gulls can be seen along the larger canals and in the docks. Occasionally, smew appear during cold spells in the winter. Males of these elegant diving ducks are most distinctive, having mainly white plumage and a bill with serrated edges for catching fish. Black redstarts can sometimes be found in parks even in the city centre. These little birds have dark plumage and a red tail. The Waterland or Zaanstreek lies to the north of the city and harbours wetland birds. Naardermeer, 9 miles (15km) to the east of Amsterdam is a wetland reserve. Write for permits to Vereniging tot Behoud can Natuurmonumenten, Herengracht 540, Amsterdam.

Woodland and Heathland

You do not have to travel far from Amsterdam to reach good areas of forest. For example, in the woods around Harderwijk, only 18 miles (30km) east of the city, you can find interesting birds.

By travelling further afield to the national park areas of De Hoge Veluwe and Veluwezoom, both

Sea holly likes to grow in the more sheltered areas of sand dunes.

north of Arnhem, you can reach more impressive areas of ancient forest interspersed with patches of heathland. The pine and birch woodland have a wide variety of fungi, especially in the autumn, and the birdlife is some of the richest in the whole country.

De Hoge Veluwe lies northwest of Arnhem near Hoenderloo. To reach it from Amsterdam drive east towards Apeldoorn and then southeast to Hoenderloo or aim for Edo and drive northeast. Veluwezoom lies 3 miles (5km) east of De Hoge Veluwe.

As dusk approaches, a woodland walk can be a rather eerie experience as a chorus of nocturnal bird-song starts up. Nightjars, which nest among the heather, churr all night long and hunt for insects in the air, while woodcock fly over the clearings making their peculiar squeaking call, known as 'roding'. These dumpy waders nest among the fallen pine needles and branches, but their camouflage is so good that you will need a keen eye to spot them. It is almost impossible to flush them and they do not fly off until you are almost on top of them.

Coastal Flowers

Lying less than 18 miles (30km) away from the city, the nearest part of the North Sea coastline is an easy drive from Amsterdam. The storm-battered shores are richly endowed with sand dunes and exciting coastal flowers stretching all the way from the Hook of Holland to Den Helder and along the entire chain of the Frisian Islands.

Coastal flowers have to be

PEACE AND QUIET

highly specialised since they must withstand the constant salt spray carried by onshore winds. The salt and the wind itself have a profound desiccating effect upon the plants which is compounded by their growing on extremely well-draining soils. Occasionally they are even inundated by seawater, something which would kill most terrestrial plants.

For the plants that grow along the Dutch coast, the sand and shingle are not a stable environment. The wind is constantly shifting the sand, either burying the plants or exposing their roots. Consequently, most of the coastal plants grow quickly and have extensive root systems which not only give them anchorage but also help them acquire water. Their leaves are often fleshy and waxy to help resist the drying effect of wind and salt and even their seeds are specially adapted. Many are completely resistant to seawater and can float, being carried by the tides to suitable beaches. One of the first plants to colonise the sand and shingle is sea rocket, which has subtle mauve flowers. It often grows with prickly saltwort, with its spiny-tipped succulent leaves, along the tideline of the highest spring tides. Above the tidelines, the plants often appear to be growing out of bare sand, but in reality they make use of the buried humus from previous strandlines. The beautiful, chamomile-like flowers of sea mayweed often grow in profusion along the strandlines. Higher up the beach, the succulent leaves of sea sandwort often form low-growing carpets over stable areas of rock and sand, while yellow-horned poppy, with its bright yellow flowers and long seed pods, nods in the breeze. The aptly named sea holly, with its prickly leaves and bracts, is often quite common and, despite its appearance, is in fact an umbellifer, more closely related to hogweed than to the thistles it resembles.

Waddenzee

Within the protection of the natural sea defences formed by the Frisian Islands lies an extensive area of calmer water called the Waddenzee. As the sea retreats on a falling tide it leaves extensive sandbanks and mudflats which at low tide cover an area of almost 1,000 square miles (2,600 sq km).

The mudflats are exceptionally rich in marine life with immense numbers of lugworms, ragworms, bivalve molluscs and other marine invertebrates. This bonanza inevitably attracts birdlife in abundance and tens, if not hundreds, of thousands of gulls, waders and wildfowl gather. The marine life of the mudflats not only supplies the breeding birds of the region but also attracts huge congregations of autumn migrants and wintering species, and supports feeders which specialise in everything from invertebrates to fish.

The waders are at their most impressive during late summer and autumn when dunlin, redshank, knot, grey plover, godwits and curlew are joined

Yellow horned poppy is one of the showiest of sand dune plants. It takes its name from its immensely long seed pods

by less numerous species such as stints, greenshank and spotted redshank. When disturbed or when flying to roost, the vast wader flocks are an impressive spectacle. Common and black-headed gulls are always in attendance, hoping to supplement their diet with a meal stolen from an unfortunate wader.

The numbers of ducks and geese are also impressive on the Waddenzee. The most conspicuous species is the shelduck, a largely black and white duck which breeds on the dunes surrounding the mudflats and which feeds by filtering the mud for small molluscs. In autumn and winter they are joined by brent geese, which despite the size that their name implies, are no bigger than the shelducks. Their main food is eel-grass, which is dying out in the Waddenzee and hence adversely affecting the numbers of geese in the area. In the deeper channels and open water, mergansers, scoters and eiders dive for fish and marine molluscs.

Until recently, common seals were a feature of the Waddenzee and Frisian Islands. Their numbers are now sadly being depleted by a virus and it can only be hoped that they begin to develop an immunity before their numbers decline too far. To reach the nearest part of the Waddenzee, drive north from Amsterdam on the N7 to Hippolytushoef and then head west towards Den Helder. View from the road.

PEACE AND QUIET

Flevoland in Winter

Traditionally, winter has not been considered the best time of year to visit the Netherlands, but with the advent of bargain breaks, out of season trips are becoming more and more popular. Lying within easy reach of Amsterdam, Flevoland's polders, dykes and fields present an unrivalled spectacle for the birdwatcher with tens of thousands of geese, swans and ducks to be seen.

Flevoland's existence is due entirely to the efforts of man. It is an area of reclaimed land in the IJsselmeer, itself formed in 1932 by the enclosure of Zuiderzee. Because the process of reclamation is continuing all the time, polders of different ages occur with habitats ranging from mud to reedbed to established grazing pasture.

The land is criss-crossed by dykes which, in cold weather, provide a good elevated position from which to watch birds in the fields. Winter is the time for geese: white-fronted geese predominate with smaller numbers of pinkfoots and bean geese.

Occasionally greylags, whose numbers peak during their August migration, linger on as well.

Thousands of Bewick's swans also visit Flevoland, sometimes joined by whoopers. Individual birds can be tricky to identify, but side-by-side the whooper is much the larger of the two, and its larger bill shows more yellow. Flocks of swans are often joined by smaller wildfowl, and pintail, wigeon and pochard are common. The first 'skeins' of geese appear in the autumn and numbers build up to a maximum by January. If it is a mild winter then the numbers may be low, the birds having remained further north.

However, if the temperatures suddenly drop then there will be an influx of geese and swans as they head south. If Flevoland itself becomes trapped in severe weather then the flocks

These Bewick's swans are among the thousands upon thousands of birds that make Flevoland a birdwatcher's paradise in winter

often desert the fields and head for southern and western Europe, and England in particular.

To reach Flevoland, head east from Amsterdam on the A1 and turn north on the A6, which crosses the area. The road between Harderwijk and Lelystad (N302), and minor roads, can be good for birds. Oostvaardersplassen is on the southwest edge of Lelystad. The Harderbroek marshes are just to the north of Harderwijk. Access is beside the Harderhaven Bridge.

Grazing Pastures
Much of the agricultural land around Amsterdam is used as grazing pasture and lies on ancient polders, many of which are actually below sea level. With the constant threat of inundation, the water levels have to be maintained and so the familiar windmill landscape has developed. Nowadays, however, much of the windmills' work has been taken over by electric pumps. There are fine meadows all around Amsterdam, some of which are even within the city boundaries.

PEACE AND QUIET

However, a short drive north from the city to Waterland or south to Biesbosch near Rotterdam will reveal a greater variety of wildlife.

Zanstreek, or Waterland, is a reserve just north of Amsterdam. It can be overlooked from the towpath which starts near the water tower in the village of Westzaan. Because the grazing pastures are composed mainly of grass, the vegetation is rather uniform and not of any special botanical interest.

Pastures and ditches such as these in Friesland make fine habitats for many species of bird, especially waders

Black-tailed godwits are noisy and conspicuous residents of the pastures. These long-billed, long-legged waders nest in grassy tussocks and are frequently seen perching on fence-posts.

March and April see the arrival of a colourful little migrant from southern Europe and Africa. In this part of Europe the yellow wagtail occurs as a blue-headed race and dazzling males can be seen in aerial battles which help settle territorial disputes.

Texel

The magical island of Texel is southernmost in the Frisian chain and is renowned throughout Europe for the variety and numbers of birds that it holds. It is within easy reach of Amsterdam, and although small in area, has a wide variety of habitats and 19 nature reserves.

Sand dunes face the North Sea gales and behind them pine woodlands help establish a stable soil system. Grazing fields, lakes and marshes all add to the interest of Texel. Although some of the island is closed for the summer to protect nesting birds, plenty can still be seen from the roads and areas of public access.

The dunes have an excellent variety of flowers, with sea rocket and sea holly abundant along the shore. Inland, marram grass helps establish the dunes and large colonies of common and black-headed gulls and terns nest in the shelter of the dune slacks.

Kentish plovers are a speciality of Texel, having disappeared from most other areas of northern Europe and long-since ceased to breed in the English county which gave them their name. Shelducks use abandoned rabbit burrows to rear their broods. Where pines have been planted or have become established, golden orioles and icterine warblers nest. Long-eared owls are also here but are difficult to see. Look for the tell-tale whitewash of droppings at the base of tree and then scan the branches for the motionless owl.

Black Tern

Black terns are summer visitors to the Netherlands, flying south in the autumn to spend the winter in Africa. They are aptly named, with greyish plumage and black head and underparts in the breeding season. In the winter, the underparts become white although they retain a black cap. The wings are slender with pointed tips and the tail is slightly forked. Unlike other terns, black terns seldom dive to feed. Instead they hunt flying insects and pick creatures from the surface of the water. The flight is elegant and graceful. They often feed and migrate in small flocks. Black terns nest in marshy areas sometimes quite close to Amsterdam. They prefer areas such as islands of floating vegetation or boggy mires, since this gives them a degree of protection from ground predators. The brood normally comprises two or three young.

Many of Texel's lakes are reed-fringed and have a rich variety of aquatic life, which in turn provides food for many wading birds such as avocet and spoonbill.

The grazing pastures on Texel have all the species of wader found elsewhere in the Netherlands. Black-tailed godwits, redshank, snipe and oystercatcher are all common and crakes and rails lurk in the ditches. During the autumn and winter, the meadows play host to flocks of wildfowl, especially at high tide, and wigeon and brent geese can be numerous. To reach Texel, drive north towards Den Helder and catch a ferry. On Texel, many people hire bikes to get around and most species can be seen from roads and tracks. There are several reserves for which permits are required. Write to the Tourist Office, Groeneplaats 9, Den Burg, Texel, or to Vereniging tot Behoud van Natuurmonumenten, Herengracht 540, Amsterdam for details.

Lakes

The west of the Netherlands is fortunate in having plenty of lakes, some of which are within easy reach of Amsterdam. To the north, the Zwanenwater lies on the route to Texel and is a coastal dune lake, while to the south, Nieuwkoop is large and reed-fringed.

Depending upon the age and size of the lakes, they will have varying mixtures of aquatic plants and animals and ones with extensive reedbeds are

PEACE AND QUIET

often important nesting sites for birds. If they have been established for a long time, a good fish population will have developed with big ruffe, perch and pike being active predators. The thriving fish populations support a wealth of fish-eating birds which nest around the lake margins. To avoid competing directly for food, each species of bird feeds in a slightly different way.

Cormorants and black-necked grebes both dive in order to catch their food, but the former catches much larger fish than the latter. Bitterns prefer to wade in the shallows and wait for fish to swim within range. These large waterbirds are more frequently heard than seen, the males 'booming' in the springtime to advertise their territories. Their diminutive relative, the little bittern, about the size of a moorhen, also haunts the reedbed margins of many lakes. Although rather shy, they are sometimes seen flying over the reeds when their pale wing panels make identification easy.

Some of the lake birds feed only on water plants, while others have a more mixed diet. The red-crested pochard, for example, dives deeply and takes aquatic vegetation from the bottom but supplements its diet with small fish, tadpoles and insects. Zwanenwater lies north of Amsterdam near Callantsoog. Explore the minor roads in the area. Nieuwkoop is south of Amsterdam near Naaden. To reach it take the A2 south, turn west onto the N201 and then south on the N212.

Polders

The process of enclosing the sea, draining the water and reclaiming the land has been going on for centuries in the Netherlands and much of the existing countryside would have been under the sea even a hundred years ago. The enclosed land is known as a 'polder' and the process continues today with the most

Bitterns spend most of their time lurking among reeds, but sometimes they step into the open, revealing wonderful, cryptic plumage

notable examples being found on the ever-growing Flevoland. After the water has been drained from the land, the ground is seeded with reeds to stabilise the soil. The variety of wetland habitats that are formed as a result, although only temporary, attracts all sorts of wildlife and makes important areas for breeding birds. On the open ground, common terns and avocets make their nest scrapes, while older reedbeds are the haunt of bearded tits. These delightful little birds look rather like feather dusters with

their plump, round bodies and long tails. Their explosive, high-pitched calls have earned them the nick-name 'pingers' and after hearing them it is not difficult to understand why. Bearded tits weave their nests among the stems of the reeds and share this habitat with reed and great reed warblers. Both these species are marvellous songsters as they cling to the highest reed stems. Dense reedbeds provide perfect cover for nesting marsh harriers, shy birds which are easily disturbed. They are common

here and the wealth of small birds and mammals ensures a good success rate for their young. As succession takes place in the polders, meadows replace the reedbeds and small mammals move in to feast on the grass roots and shoots. Both short-tailed and ground voles can reach plague proportions and inevitably attract large numbers of birds of prey. Day-hunting short-eared owls and hen harriers quarter the ground and often stay to breed. During the winter months, rough legged buzzards supplement their numbers and take a great toll on the voles. The polders of the Netherlands are possibly the best place in Europe to see these graceful raptors and up to 100 in a day can be seen on Flevoland alone in a good year. Even at a distance, they are easy to identify because they have a conspicuous white rump and a habit of hovering, an unusual feat for so large a bird.

Marshes

Despite the managed nature of much of the countryside around Amsterdam, in some areas, wetlands have developed into superb marshes. Gnarled willows and tangled wetland undergrowth provide cover for secretive birds and mammals and many species nest here. In some areas, such as Biesbosch near Rotterdam, the trees support breeding colonies of night herons. As their name suggests, they are nocturnal, spending the day roosting in the trees, and flying out at night to feed in the pools, lakes and ditches.

Where they are not disturbed or polluted, ditches and canals have an interesting variety of emergent water plants such as flowering rush and branched bur-reed. If sufficient cover develops, the ditches become the haunt of the shy water rail. Although they prefer to breed in extensive reedbeds, outside the breeding season water rails are found in all sorts of watery places, and ditches are a favourite winter site unless they freeze over.

Water rails are secretive birds, but give their presence away

---

The Ruff

Ruffs are elegant wading birds with yellow legs and a rather small head for the size of the body. They are locally common breeding birds in the marshes of the Netherlands, often nesting close to the outskirts of Amsterdam. They have an upright stance and males earn their name from the 'ruff' of feathers which adorn their napes and ear coverts during the breeding season. These ruffs may be black, white or chestnut; females lack them altogether and are known as 'reeves'. At the start of the breeding season, males congregate on traditional sites known as 'leks' where they display and battle for the attentions of the females. In flight, they can be recognised by the narrow wing bar and by the pattern on the rump, which has a black central band and white patches on the side.

Pool frogs are common marshland residents. They form a substantial part of the diet of such birds as herons and bitterns

with their loud, pig-like squeals. If you hear this sound then sit quietly beside the ditch or pool and wait: sooner or later the bird will emerge from cover. If you lose patience, try making a squeaking sound with a blade of grass because this sometimes fools the bird into thinking there is a rival in the vicinity and it temporarily forgets its natural shyness. Where marshes grade into managed flood meadows this provides a perfect habitat for ruffs.

Birds of the Coast

The extensive coastline of the Netherlands is very attractive to birds. There is something to see all through the year with breeding birds in the summer, migrants in spring and autumn and winter specialities along the beaches.

During the summer months, the coasts teem with vast numbers of breeding terns and gulls. Herring, black-headed and common gulls all form noisy colonies and sometimes are joined by nesting terns. Sadly, little and sandwich terns are no longer numerous, but common terns form large colonies, laying their camouflaged eggs in shallow scrapes in the sand and shingle. The young are also extremely well camouflaged and are difficult to spot, and are consequently very vulnerable to disturbance and trampling by tourists.

All the terns catch fish and can be seen diving even into

shallow water after sand eels and other small species. In the autumn, they leave Europe to migrate south for the winter, often flying in the company of other seabirds like shearwaters and skuas. These species, which spend most of their lives far from land, are most frequently seen during periods of onshore gales in September and October. September and October can witness huge 'falls' of songbirds, with flocks – hundreds or thousands strong – of bramblings, twites and snow buntings. At this time of year there is always a chance of an unusual bird coming in with one of these flocks. Bluethroats and barred warblers are regularly seen, looking most out of place among the maritime plants. Some of the snow buntings stay for the winter and may be joined by shore larks, While shore larks creep around slowly and are sometimes difficult to see, the flocks of snow buntings burst into the air with jingling calls and flashing white patches on their wings.

Almost any unspoilt spot along the coast from the Hook of Holland to Den Helder is likely to be good for flowers and birds. However, De Kennemerduinen National Park, near Haarlem, is particularly worth visiting. There are footpaths, campsites, two car parks and an information centre. Access is from the towns of Bergen and Alkmaar. There are sand dunes, freshwater marshes and shallow lakes. Good for coastal flora and migrant birds.

Bulb Fields

From March to May, the fields around Amsterdam become a kaleidoscope of colourful flowers. These are the famous bulbfields. Some of the best areas in the country lie between Leiden and Haarlem, within easy reach of the city. A day's driving along the dykes overlooking the bulbfields is a memorable experience, and the railway journey across the bulbfields also affords lovely views.

Bulbs act as underground 'food stores' for many different plants – the most famous being tulips – and give the plants a 'head-start' over herbaceous plants, allowing them to flower much earlier. Also flowering in the early spring are the fruit trees, whose pink and white blossoms are a subtle contrast to the sometimes gaudy bulb flowers. Although tulips are the most commonly cultivated bulbs, gladiolus, narcissus, lily, iris, hyacinth and crocus are also grown, The cultivation and world-wide export of bulbs from the Netherlands is a major industry.

If you make a spring visit to see the bulb fields, be sure to see the gardens at Keukenhof, near Lisse. They are an easy drive from Amsterdam and form the largest bulb flower gardens in the world. In the 70 acres (28ha) of land, 6 to 7 million bulbs are reckoned to be planted each year – so it is no wonder that the gardens are a riot of colour in the spring!

Schiphol Airport's duty free shops are extensive and for certain items may be better than the shops in central Amsterdam

SHOPPING

Shopping in Amsterdam can be divided into two parts – the city and the airport. You can do very well with certain items at Schiphol, so it is probably worth checking on what is available there before you splash out in the city centre. In the central city everything is in easy walking reach and offers possibilities for all purses from luxury to budget. There are major department stores selling all the smart items of clothes, records, perfumes, jewellery, linens and china (much specifically Dutch so of interest to tourists, but of course many imported goods too for the local market) and also hundreds of small speciality shops. The main streets are the two long thoroughfares, the Kalverstraat and the Nieuwendijk; and the Leidsestraat with its small shops mingled with cafés is also a walking street, although the trams and bikes whoosh down it so you must not cross without looking first!

Appropriately for a city which has always been a trading centre, Amsterdam is a producer of many things, but most notable commodities are flowers and bulbs, diamonds, agricultural products, vegetables, cheeses and chocolate as well as handicraft items from woven blankets to wooden clogs, furniture and pottery. Luxury goods include fashion items and furs, pictures and sculptures, and antiquities – there is a special area of the city for fashion (around the Museumplein) and for antiques (the Spiegelkwartier, by the Rijksmuseum).

Books

The main area for books is around the university district off the Spui and the Leidsestraat. Not all books are in Dutch – there are foreign language sections and English is well represented both in new and old bookstores. You are usually very welcome to browse.

Book Market An interesting excursion can be made to the book market on the street known as the Oudemanhuispoort. Small secondhand shops, stalls and tables piled with volumes make this little street a fascinating place to visit on a sunny day.

American Discount Book Center Kalverstraat 185: A large store with many English volumes, a typical sort of cut-price place, breezy and modern. There is a so-called English tea-room here, Lindsay's, for a break between browsing, or to examine purchases.

Athenaeum Bockhandel, Spui 14-16: A longstanding shop, well known in the city with interesting architectural features distinguishing its corner site – note the sinuous art nouveau window frames. Helpful staff. A pleasant sitting area close by is near the little statue of a backstreet Amsterdam boy known as 'the cheeky lad'.

Close by on NZ Voorburgwal are antique and old books at number 304, and in a leaning old house at number 330.

W H Smith is represented at Kalverstraat 152, with a comprehensive guidebook section covering Amsterdam and the Netherlands.

Newspapers and Magazines (in English and other languages): A variety can be found at AKO, Centraal Station.

Bulbs

You can find them in all sorts of small shops (try shopping along

Cheese is a staple part of the Dutch diet, often eaten at breakfast. It is sold packaged in pieces or, better, whole

the cluttered streets around the Haarlemmerdijk) or in the big stores and also at the airport. It might be best to save your bulb shopping until you make an excursion to one of the bulb-growing towns outside Amsterdam. Bulbs are sold in sacks, in paper envelopes, and loose and you may find that they can vary a lot in quality from place to place, so shop around.

Airport Duty Free, Schiphol: Not much on offer, but there are bulbs for sale, usually in small packs. You probably won't save much, but still useful for last minute presents.

Flower Market
(Bloemenmarkt), The Singel: Here in a series of stands and flat-bottomed boats moored on the canal you can buy a variety of bulbs as well as plants and flowers. They can be packed in bags, by the hundreds or by tens, and this is much the cheapest place to buy bulbs, since terms are cash only as a rule. Plenty to choose from (Monday to Saturday 09.00 to 17.00).

Cheeses

You will taste a lot of Dutch cheese on a holiday – it is even part of typical Dutch breakfasts

SHOPPING

with cold meats. You can find it packaged at any supermarket or food speciality shop, but it is best to buy a whole cheese, especially some of the aged Goudas, which are not easily obtainable outside Holland. Best way to get a cheese is at some of the cheese-towns around Amsterdam – Alkmaar, Edam and Gouda have cheese markets and plenty of possibilities for shopping in their centres. (There is a Cheese Museum at Alkmaar.)

Chocolate

There is an abundance of small chocolate shops in the city, and their sales windows can be a joy, piled with hand-made chocolates, chocolate bars, chocolate packed in Delft tile designs, marzipan animals. Try the Leidseplein for little shops. Department stores have large sections, usually on the ground floor.

Herman Kwekkeboom
Reguliersbreestraat 39: Busy crowded store on a major street, filled with all kinds of pastries and rich chocolates.

Pompadour, Huidenstraat 12: An old-fashioned shop with a well filled window. The place looks more like a salon than a chocolate shop, all articles are handsomely set out, and there is plenty to choose from.

Airport Duty Free, Plenty of choice, often special sales, from speciality shops on the main duty-free concourse. Few loose chocolates but lots of boxes and bars. Airport shops also accept credit cards.

Coffee

Dutch coffee is rich and redolent. It is usually drunk fairly strong and the taste may not be yours, yet it is still worth looking into the Amsterdam coffee shops if only for the wonderful

There is plenty of opportunity for browsing in antique shops, though genuine old Delftware and tiles command huge prices

atmosphere and aroma of blends. Teas are also sold in the coffee shops as well as machines for making coffee, etc.
Wijs Koffie, 102 Warmoesstraat: Brass-framed windows and ornate old letters tell you this is a real old-established shop, full of age and charm. The scent of the coffee seems to have seeped everywhere. You can buy it loose or ready weighed in packets.

Geels en Co, Warmoesstraat 67: Another old-timer, and a must even if you only look in the windows. Helpful in suggesting blends you may like. Modern aids for coffee-making sold. There are old tins and implements to look at.

Crafts/Antiques

Again, Dutch interest in crafts is evident in many small shops and galleries and antiques are sold from small cluttered shops in the older districts, such as the Rokin and the Spiegelkwartier (the area around the Rijksmuseum).
De Looier, Elandsgracht 109: An antique market with many small stalls, a good introduction under one roof to what the city offers to collectors or just to curio seekers. Open from 11.00 to 17.00 every day except Friday (Sunday from 12.00), free entry.
Kiek's Horloger, Leidsestraat 21: Old clocks as well as modern timepieces in a very charming old shop illuminated with chandeliers.
Amsterdam Antiques Gallery, Nieuwe Spiegelstraat 34: Ten dealers under one roof selling icons, clocks, pewter and paintings amongst other items.

Department Stores

Not many big stores in the city, though there are several small ones and open-plan shops along the main shopping streets. International chain stores for shoes, clothes, fashions and foodstuffs can be found here also.
Bijenkorf, Dam: De Bijenkorf literally means 'the beehive' and it can be as busy as that on a Saturday or during its sales. Several floors offering everything from luxuries to staples. Look for Dutch handicrafts here.
Maison de la Bonneterie, Kalverstraat 183: One of those hold-overs from an earlier age, this gracious shop is small yet smart with an old-style façade, specialising mostly in fashions.
Esprit, Spui 10: A modern store, small yet welcoming, with clothes and specialities, also a convenient and welcoming coffee bar, in the middle of the student quarter.
Metz, Keizersgracht 455: A general store in the centre of the city (off the Leidsestraat) with several floors. Wide variety of goods and a cheap, well appointed snack bar with a fine view of the city.

Diamonds

Even if you do not want to buy (and apparently there are bargains to be had) you will want to see the stones being cut and prepared in the workshops which can be found all over central Amsterdam. Entry is almost always free and you may even get free coffee too. Tours are on offer seven days a week but times vary.

SHOPPING

Wandering round flea markets is a popular Dutch pastime for all the family. Haggling with stallholders is part of the fun

Amsterdam has particularly skilled diamond cutters and the term 'Amsterdam cut' means top quality work. The Depression came down with particular force on the gem industry and then World War II meant many factories were closed or moved abroad because of the industry's many Jewish owners and skilled workers. After the war factories were concentrated in the centre – it is a clean non-polluting business – in order to be close to customers and the increasing tourist business. Many sales are now made direct to visitors, particularly the Japanese. A fascinating visit can be made with a tour guide giving a good, well delivered talk on how diamonds are mined, cut and polished, and how quality is judged as regards size, colour and clarity. Seeing the craftsmen at their benches cutting the precious stones is also intriguing.

Amsterdam Diamond Center, Rokin 1–5: One of the biggest of the diamond cutters and polishers. Slick tours around this modern operation tend to be well run, but can be crowded and commercial. (Tours take place daily from 09.30 to 17.00; from 10.30 Sundays November to March.)

Coster Diamonds, Paulus Potterstraat 2; behind Rijksmuseum: A smart mansion is the setting for diamond-viewing here, and they may ask for an identity check. Open daily 09.00 to 17.00.

Holshusen-Stoeltie, Wagenstraat 13-17 (off Amstelstraat): This small and unprepossessing firm is one of the nicest in the city. Signs are in English and the informative tour lasts about half an hour. Diamonds have been an industry in the Dutch capital since the 17th century, and one room is set up as a museum with authentic tools and a diamond mill of the period. It is very interesting to compare this with the new methods on show. After you have gazed at the sparklers in the showrooms upstairs you are invited for a free coffee at their own small coffee house across the street. (Workshop open daily 09.00 to 17.00.)

Not far from this factory is **Amstel Diamonds** at Amstel 208, a jewellers demonstrating diamond cutting.

The city's reputation for cutting and polishing diamonds is well-founded, and many visitors enjoy bargain-hunting

Van Moppes Diamonds, Albert Cuypstraat 2–6: This is one of the largest and most international of the companies, open daily, 08.30 to 17.00. You get a tour and a look (through a microscope) at the tiniest cut-diamond known. Van Moppes is located near the museum quarter.

Markets

Local markets are very popular with the Dutch – they take the children and make it an outing. Lots of stalls and spaces, a vast mixture of things on sale from worthwhile antiques and furnishings to absolute rubbish. Second-hand clothes and video material. The food stalls are

SHOPPING

good: you can get all sorts of fast-food. It's well prepared – try the crisp chips with mayonnaise. Wander about with the bustling crowd and enjoy the atmosphere.

Albert Cuypmarkt: One of the biggest and most expansive in Holland. Stalls are all along the Albert Cuypstraat off the Hobbemakade or approach via the Ruysdaelstraat. The streets round here, not far from the museum quarter, are all named after famous Dutch artists. Very much a local market with all sorts of foodstuffs as well as second-hand and new clothes. A good place too for a snack or a light lunch.

The market also overflows into the Ferdinand Bolstraat which crosses it.

Open early Monday to Saturday, the market is finished by 17.00 and everyone is packing up.

Bird Market: Around the Noorderkerk in the Jordaan on Saturday mornings. Cage-birds but also other items are on sale in the little square next to the church. The market extends down a local street, very much a neighbourhood place.

Books: second-hand volumes at Oudemanhuispoort, open Monday to Saturday.

Flower Market (Bloemenmarkt): Beside the Singel, in the centre of town. Bulbs, plants, seeds and blooms. Open Monday to Saturday 09.00 to 17.00.

Nieuwmarkt: A square that used to be a regular market, now open and tranquil – very different from wartime days when it was a centre of black-market business. There is an open-air antiques market here from mid-May to September, 10.00 to 16.00, Sundays only.

Thorbeckeplein: Off the Amstelstraat, an art market, is held mid-March to mid-December on Sundays 10.30 to 18.00.

Stamp and coin market, for specialist interests. The rather dreary Nieuwezijds Voorburgwal is enlivened on Wednesday and Saturday afternoons with dealers.

Waterlooplein: Beside the Muziektheater, a large and busy space which has been created for this Amsterdam institution after it was moved away for a period.

It lacks character in its surroundings, yet is still a lively place filled with people looking at the stands and stalls. All sorts of stuff on sale, many clothes stalls, records and videos, knick-knacks, so-called antiques (mostly junk but of course you may see a treasure). Stall-holders can be pleasant, but also surly and sometimes rude.

The food stalls are good, and cheap. Beside the Jodenbreestraat, this is one market not to miss. Open Monday to Friday 09.00 to 17.00; Saturday 08.30 to 17.30.

Shopping Centres

There are three large shopping complexes: **De Amsterdamse Poort**, reached by Metro at Amsterdam Zuid-Oost; the recently opened **Magna Plaza**, exclusive shops in a wonderful old building behind the Dam; and the **Winkelcentrum Boven't IJ**, reached by ferry across the IJ.

FOOD AND DRINK

Eating Out

There are plenty of places to eat in Amsterdam, all the way from simple cafés to expensive restaurants with lush décors. There is a wide range of cooking styles, however, from the plain and filling Dutch dishes to Oriental, Greek, American, Mexican, Italian, Egyptian, Indian and Indonesian food. You have plenty of choice, and many places take credit cards and travellers' cheques.

Wine tends to be expensive, and so are drinks in smart bars. They are much more reasonable in unprepossessing local cafés.

Dutch food is filling and sometimes heavy, with a strong accent on stews of meat or fish with vegetables, as well as hearty soups – pea soup

All fish is fresh and very good. Smoked eels are a local delicacy

(*erwtensoep*) being a favourite winter warmer, properly made with a hambone or bacon if you are lucky – accompanied by

---

Tourist Menus

Some restaurants in Holland serve a special fixed-price menu for visitors; around 280 participating establishments display a blue sign with a fork between the words 'Tourist Menu'. The menu is often created especially by the chef, and may well feature seasonal specialities. A leaflet listing all these restaurants is available from the Netherlands Board of Tourism, or local VVV offices in Amsterdam. Also, you could try one of the 110 restaurants throughout the country advertising 'Neerlands Dis'. Displaying signs of a red, white and blue soup tureen, they specialise in reasonably priced Dutch cuisine using local ingredients.

FOOD AND DRINK

hunks of crusty bread. Fish is always popular and the nearby North Sea still provides a catch, as do local waterways for eels and freshwater fish. Fish is preserved in a number of ways from smoking to salting – try a pickled herring from a corner stand if you can find one. Lots of poultry and eggs are eaten, and red meat grilled or fried. Main dishes are accompanied by mounds of vegetables and loads of potatoes, often fried. You can round off a typical Dutch meal with a large portion of good apple pie and ice cream. What Dutch food lacks in subtlety, it certainly makes up for in substance!

Sandwich bars can be found all over the city and are ideal for a light lunch. The sandwiches are called *broodjes* and are sometimes hot (*warme*). They can be on crisp white or brown bread, or on rolls both hard and soft. Wandering round markets you find many small stands selling things to eat, from fish and bread to cakes and fried potatoes. In summer people sit out with picnics on the wooden benches in certain squares and gardens.

The Dutch have a sweet tooth, so other items for immediate eating are the fluffed up *poffertjes*, the Dutch answer to doughnuts and quite delicious, as well as various cakes and pancakes, which are rolled up and filled with creams and jams (and can also have cheese or meat fillings as a main course). The chocolate and sweet shops are wonderful just to look at, and serve a variety of chocolates and goods made of marzipan.

An Indonesian rice-table, popular with the Dutch whose links with Indonesia date back to 300 years of colonialism

Dutch chocolate is very good. Dutch coffee is hot and strong, usually freshly made. For breakfast in hotels you will usually be offered coffee or tea (or hot chocolate) and then a range of cold meats and cheeses, or scrambled eggs, sausages, bacon at some places. There will be plenty of breads, and (increasingly) wholefood cereals with dried fruit and nuts, as well as a range of yoghurts.

Cheap sandwich joints abound in central Amsterdam with hamburger chains in all the major streets – fast, filling and very popular with teenagers and children. Hardly adventurous but useful if you

The Indonesian Connection

Indonesian food is much appreciated and it comes to Amsterdam through earlier colonial connections – many Indonesians settled in the city after the one-time colonies became independent. You certainly should try an exotic rice table (*rijsttafel*) with its many dishes and pile of rice to eat with them, and you will also get *satay* or skewers of meat chunks which have been prepared in peanut oil.
The dishes are very varied and are not usually too highly spiced.
As with Indian food it is probably best to drink a light Dutch beer with this kind of a meal, since wine rarely goes well with such strong and unusual flavours.

are in a hurry or do not really care what you eat. Department stores and museums have good quality cafeterias that are inexpensive. Those on a budget might prefer to try a pizzeria – you can find them in central streets usually tricked out like an Italian restaurant, so the atmosphere is not as plastic as the American-style cafés. Wine is served and a whole pizza, with salad and the trimmings, plus drinks should not be more than 22 guilders for two and you will not be hurried out, so you can linger over your coffee (which is cheap in most places in Amsterdam). You may also want to explore less expensive snack-type restaurants and these can be found in department stores (such as Metz, Keisersgracht 455, 5th floor) or along central streets (try Berkhoff, Leidsestraat 46, or Pompadour, Huidenstraat 12) or you can try traditional light dishes such as pancakes at the Pancake Bakery, Prinsengracht 191, where you will find dozens of varieties of the *pannekoeken*. If you are a vegetarian then Holland welcomes you with plenty of possibilities, from buffets offering mounds of salads, to speciality restaurants. Oriental and Indian restaurants will often have vegetable dishes. Kosher food can also be found. If you want special foods then it is wise to check before you go for a list of places from the tourist offices, or ask at the VVV when you arrive.

Drinking
The traditional place to drink in Amsterdam is at the 'brown

FOOD AND DRINK

Café society is relaxed, friendly and caters for all tastes

bars' (named for the tobacco which seems to have invaded the very woodwork of some of the older ones, leaving a dark brown patina). These can be found all over the city, often crowded with local people at busy times such as the end of afternoon, but usually friendly. As in Germany, brewing of beer is a national skill. There are big breweries in the city; one of the largest is Heineken's, on the Stadhouderskade. The competitor, Amstel, is almost as large and you will see advertising signs for the two brews all over the country as well as other less well known ones. Brouwhuis Maiximiliaan, near Nieumarkt, brews three types of beer (plus seasonal varieties) which you can try in the café here. Bars will sell beers either in bottle or on tap with the latter being cheaper. Beer is sometimes drunk with Jenever gin, the Dutch variety of the spirit and very cheap at duty free areas and in shops if you happen to like the fiery taste. It does not mix well and is almost always drunk on its own in tiny tumblers.

Wine is obtainable easily in Amsterdam, but is better drunk in good quality restaurants with a good list. Wine bars are still rare, but you can find modern bars serving cocktails and beer, usually in stark designs and with loud music and discreet lighting. In general, a café or brown bar is more atmospheric.

In summer people take their drinks outside and some of the bars have little terraces on the canals.

Coffee is an urban necessity in Amsterdam and almost anywhere will allow you to either sit at a table with a coffee or stand at the bar and just have a cup.

Restaurants

Dutch
The following all display the sign of the 'dis' – a red, white and blue soup tureen to show that traditional Dutch cooking is served (see page 85).
Bodega Keyzer, van Baerlestraat 96 (tel: 6711441). This 'bodega' is an Amsterdam institution. It is near the Concertgebouw and attracts

patrons to its terrace and cosy café atmosphere. Go for a drink or for a meal, but you may need to book in the evening.

Brasserie de Roode Leeuw (Hotel de Roode Leeuw), Damrak 93-94 (tel: 6240396). Set close to the entertainment centre of the city, this restaurant specialises in solid Dutch food. Its reasonable prices make it popular with locals.

Poort Restaurant (Hotel de Port van Cleve), NZ Voorburgwal 178 (tel: 6240047). A restaurant of atmosphere with wooden panelling and tile mural. This is a place to try old-style Dutch cooking with many special dishes such as the famed pea soup, stews, sauerkraut and boiled puddings.

Visrestaurant 'Julia', Amstelveenseweg 160 (tel: 6795394). A noted fish restaurant offering fresh as well as smoked and cured fish.

Dutch and International
De Groene Lanteerne, Haarlemmerstraat 43 (tel: 6241952). Very much a neighbourhood place, long and very narrow, 300-year-old room offering Dutch dishes and French cuisine as well.

De Nachtwacht, Thorbeckeplein 2 (tel: 6224794). Right in the nightclub district near Rembrandtplein, it is a smart place with many dishes featuring steak and sea foods. Reasonably priced.

D'Vijf Vlieghen (The Five Flies), Spuistraat 294 (tel: 6248369). A famous old place this, a warren of rooms, rambling through several houses and with unusual period decors and much good old furniture and decorative items. Note the etchings, said to be Rembrandt originals. Expensive, but an experience. Dutch and French.

French
Beddington's, Roelof Hartstraat 6 (tel: 6765201). Decor at this cool, modern restaurant may at first appear a little austere, but there is always a warm welcome. The food is highly imaginative, cooking very competent, and presentation quite artistic. Booking essential. Closed Sunday.

Christophe, Leliegracht 46 (tel: 6250807). A relatively new restaurant but already a great success. Situated on one of the small canals behind the Westerkerk in the Jordaan area, this spacious restaurant is cool, comfortable, and tastefully decorated. The menu offers light and stylish cooking at surprisingly reasonable prices, and in generous portions. It's a very popular place and is often crowded after 21.00 so late diners should book well in advance. Closed Sunday and Monday.

Excelsior (Hôtel de l'Europe), Nieuwe Doelenstraat 2-8 (tel: 6234836). Situated right in the heart of Amsterdam, this elegant restaurant has superb views over the river Amstel, the flower market and the Munttoren. Impeccable service, old-world ambience, mainly classical French dishes prepared in an imaginative, quite modern style. There is an emphasis on seafood.

De Kersentuin (Garden Hotel)

FOOD AND DRINK

Dijsselhofplantsoen 7 (tel: 6642121). This is undoubtedly one of the most elegant restaurants in town. *Kersentuin* means cherry orchard, hence the slight Japanese touch as well as the red cherry in the aperitifs and on the china. A slight Italian bias, so there is excellent pasta. The lounge often features modern art exhibitions, fashion shows, and other such events. Booking necessary, Closed Sunday.

De Trechter, Hobbemakade 63 (tel: 6711263). Small and modest, this restaurant is now considered one of the best in Amsterdam. The decor is simple, the atmosphere cosy, and the quality of food outstanding. Speciality is smoked food. There are only eight tables so book well in advance.

Tout Court, Runstraat 13 (tel: 6258637). Small and cosy, slightly bohemian. Excellent French cuisine bourgeoise. Loyal guests include musicians who come here to enjoy their favourite dishes after the evening's concert. Always crowded, so book in advance. Closed Sunday and Monday.

Health Food
Manna Natuurvoeding, Spui No 1, Haarlemmendijk (tel: 6253743).
More of a shop and snack bar, but worth noting for those who do not want a meat diet which often seems hard to avoid in hearty-eating Amsterdam. Centrally placed. The tables in the gallery offer a range of vegetarian cooking and there is a take-out service.

Indian
Koh-I-Noor, Westermarkt 29 (tel: 6233133). This is a very good restaurant, centrally placed and deservedly popular. It suggests reasonably priced set menus as well as classic Indian dishes. Good portions and good value – hence it is usually busy so make reservations.

Indonesian
Padi Mas, PC Hooftstraat 87 (tel: 6646421). A popular Indonesian restaurant within the Memphis Hotel, offering good food at reasonable prices.

Speciaal, Nieuwe Leliestraat 142 (tel: 6249706). Indonesian food is one of the delights of Amsterdam, the many

restaurants showing connections forged in the colonial era. This one is small, a bit off the track, yet worthwhile and reasonable.

Mexican
Rose's Cantina
Reguliersdwarsstraat 38 (tel: 6259797). A fashionable place, since Mexican food is very modish with the young trendies of Amsterdam. It is also pretty authentic here, and cheap. Very crowded, however, so expect to wait.

Oriental
China Treasure, NZ Voorburgwal 115 (tel: 6260915). Chinese specialities include Pekinese food in this authentic restaurant which is not a cheap place to eat – rather the reverse, in fact. But there is a selection of good and well prepared dishes.

Dynasty, Reguliersdwarsstraat 30 (tel: 6268400). A most elegant, exotic restaurant: orchids, golden Buddhas and Thai silk hangings adorn the interior, and there is a stylish little garden for dinner outside on fine summer evenings. Service is perfect, and the refined cooking features dishes of southeast Asia, Malaysian dishes and good classic Cantonese, Thai and Vietnamese food based on

One of Amsterdam's numerous Indonesian restaurants

FOOD AND DRINK

lobster, prawns, fish, lamb and pork.

Seafood

Bols Taverne, Rozengracht 106 (tel: 6245752). This is a stylish and popular restaurant, an old warehouse which is decorated throughout with a sea and sailing decor in its rooms. Naturally fish and seafood are the staples, but you can also get meat such as steak, and bar meals too. Closed Sunday.

Lucius, Spuistraat 247 (tel: 6241831). A very agreeable and cosy place this, with atmospheric interiors and a style of its own. Speciality is fish, with a large selection moderately priced, and a variety of unusual desserts.

Le Pêcheur, Reguliersdwarsstraat 32 (tel: 6243121). The setting evokes a 1920s Paris bistro at this simple but very good fish restaurant. The fish is outstandingly fresh and beautifully cooked, with interesting, light sauces. The restaurant is situated behind the flower market in a trendy street full of popular eating places, and in summer you can eat out in the small garden at the back.

Outside Amsterdam

Auberge De Nederlanden, Duinkerken 3, Vreeland (tel: 02943-1576). Old country inn on the pretty shores of the river Vecht, where in the 18th century the rich merchants of Amsterdam built their mansions and summer houses. The menu is seasonal; the cooking light and very good. There's also a bistro.

Bistro Klein Paardenburg, Amstelzijde 59, Ouderkerk aan de Amstel (tel: 02963-1335). About 6 miles (10km) from Amsterdam, in a quiet village on the River Amstel, this small country inn offers marvellous food, combining a great deal of imagination with a classic touch. Salmon, Dutch lamb, seafood and fantastic salads. Home-style sweets, outstanding Dutch cheeses. Very popular, so book well in advance.

De Bokkedoorns, Zeeweg 53, Overveen (tel: 023-263600). One of the best restaurants in the Netherlands, De Bokkedoorns stands in a peaceful lakeside setting of dunes and woodland about 15 miles (25km) from Amsterdam. Wonderful fresh food which varies according to seasons: morels from the dunes, grilled scallops, tender Dutch lamb and unusual game dishes. Very good sweets too. There is an attractive light lunch menu and in summer you can dine on the terrace. Booking recommended, especially at the weekends.

Molen 'De Dikkert', Amsterdamseweg 104, Amstelveen (tel: 6411378). De Dikkert (meaning the big one) is a majestic old windmill right in the middle of a village on the outskirts of Amsterdam. It forms the setting for this stylish restaurant, popular with the international business community (there's even a menu in Japanese). This is the place for the best Dutch products – veal and lamb, seafood and asparagus, oysters and smoked eel. An impressive wine list includes a good choice of half-bottles.

The range of accommodation in Amsterdam is wide – from luxury hotels to basic youth hostels

ACCOMMODATION

You will find in Amsterdam an amazingly wide variety of places to stay, from hotels of great luxury and style to cheap budget accommodation of shared rooms or dormitories. Many small and reasonable hotels are in the centre, clustered along the canals, concentrated in such areas as the Leidseplein. Many are in old houses, redolent with the Dutch charm of hanging plants, pottery and a cosy element of clutter. The Dutch passion for cleanliness is usually evident in sparkling brass, copper and glass and there is a definite air of homeliness.

Old houses in the city, with their steep staircases, wide windows and cheerful neighbourliness are very pleasant places to stay, some of them with canal views.

Bedrooms may not be large in older places, but you can usually be sure of a very comfortable bed in a warm yet not overheated house with the personal attention of the owners from the time you check in.

The bigger hotels are scattered around the city centre and the airport. There is a wide selection and while expensive they are not as dear as in some other cities. Some are conventional chain-type hotels, others are unusual both architecturally and from a service point of view. (Note the Pulitzer and the American hotels, both deservedly landmarks of hospitality in this city and well worth considering if you want something different at a luxury price.) Needless to say all take credit cards, and offer the usual range of top-class service.

Some have particularly good places to eat and some are noted as being places to which stars and royalty are drawn. (Note the Amstel Inter Continental facing the river.) Anyone visiting Amsterdam will want to be in the middle, and you have a range of places to choose from in the centre.

You may save money by staying the suburbs, but usually the inconvenience is not worth the small saving. Package tour companies usually offer a variety of hotels. An excellent one is Travelscene, but you could also try Time Off or book through Winter, the Amsterdam Way, a service of the Netherlands Reservation Centre

ACCOMMODATION

(see page 95), and a winter-only deal. This can be checked out with the Netherlands Board of Tourism or the VVV Amsterdam Tourist Office. It offers a range of hotels at various prices as well as a number of free items from canal cruises to museum entries and free drinks, plus reductions on numerous other attractions. The scheme operates from 1 November to 31 March and more information is available from the Netherlands Reservation Centre itself.

In most hotels except the very expensive you will be provided with a typical Dutch breakfast, sometimes in buffet-style but often served to you at the table. It will always feature cold meats, thinly sliced cheese (Dutch of course), boiled eggs and a variety of breads and toasts. More and more hot dishes of eggs, bacon, sausage and ham are available, so you can make a full meal of your breakfast, which comes of course with strong coffee, tea or hot chocolate, and sometimes cereals, juices and yoghurts to start with. If you eat heartily you will not want to spend much time lunching, and this will give you added hours to sightsee.

If your dinner is typical you will get hearty helpings – another

The American Hotel, just off the Leidseplein, is in the deluxe class and with its Art Nouveau features is a city landmark

good reason for making your lunches in Amsterdam light and sensible!

Do not automatically expect a private shower or bath in this city – ask if you do need private facilities, otherwise you may have to share a bathroom with a neighbour or two. This is not usually too inconvenient, but check when you book.

Reservations

Remember that in the summer, at Christmas and New Year, and during such busy tourist times as the tulip season (April–May), hotels can be very busy and you may not have a wide choice. Prices vary by season, but not usually by very much. It is always wiser to have accommodation booked ahead at busy periods, if only for your own peace of mind. Amsterdam does have a high rate of turnover, however, so you will usually be accommodated even if it does mean waiting around sometimes.

VVV Accommodation Service (**Logiesservice**) This is intended for people who are already in the country and need assistance in finding accommodation. VVV offices (there are more than 120 of them in Holland) offer same-day bookings, either for a night or subsequent nights for a small charge.

From VVV offices outside Amsterdam bookings for accommodation in the city can be made by visiting the local office (not by telephoning) and suggestions will be made depending on availability. Reservations for accommodation can be made at any VVV office bearing the blue and white sign 'i-Nederland' with a large distinctive 'i'. Another service run by the VVV is a programme that introduces visitors to local families.

Netherlands Reservation Centre (NRC) PO Box 404, 2260 AK Leidschendam; the Netherlands. A useful and efficient free national booking service for all kinds of accommodation from leading hotels to typical Dutch log cabins in the country. Reservations can be made in writing, by telephone (070-3202500) or fax (070-3202611) – no personal callers. Confirmation of your booking will be made either in writing or by fax.

Hotels

If you are telephoning from outside Amsterdam in the Netherlands, the code is 020. **American** Leidsekade 97 (tel: 6245322), 4-star, 188 rooms. A fine example of early 20th-century styles with red brick, stained glass, tiles and plaster decoration.

The Café Américain on the ground floor is a landmark with geometrical lighting fixtures and reading tables littered with magazines and newspapers. **AMS Museum Hotel** PC Hooftstraat 2 (tel: 6621402), 3-star, very comfortable, 110 rooms. A medium priced hotel on the edge of the museum district, old-style classic looks. 'Brown' bar.

Amstel Inter Continental Prof Tulpplein 1 (tel: 6226060), 5-star, 79 rooms. Known as the

ACCOMMODATION

queen of Amsterdam's hotels this is an old-style grand hostelry recently renovated. Facing the wide Amstel, a little out of the centre, yet accessible, it is a favoured place for local special events and visiting dignitaries. Terrace and a noble stone stair in the foyer.

Amsterdam Hilton, Apollolaan 138 (tel: 6780780), 5-star, hotel with 271 rooms. A typical Hilton, large and streamlined, just beyond the centre. Wide views.

Amsterdam Marriott Stadhouderskade 12 (tel: 6075555), 5-star, 392 rooms. A handsome new construction, well placed for the Leidseplein and the museums.

Amsterdam Wiechmann Prinsengracht 328 (tel: 6263321), 2-star, comfortable, 36 rooms. A bargain hotel of character on a canal, furnished with antiques, quiet and central.

Canal House Keizersgracht 148 (tel: 6225182), 3-star 'comfortable' hotel, 26 rooms. A small yet perfectly charming, old-style hotel with antiques and an elegant air.

Forte Crest Apollo Apollolaan 2 (tel: 6735922), 5-star, 228 rooms. Ultra modern, just beyond the centre, overlooking the water with café terraces; most rooms are in a low-rise block.

Garden Dijsselhofplantsoen 7 (tel: 6642121), 5-star, 98 rooms. Beside a waterway near the Apollolaan and handy for the museums and the Vondelpark. Features the award-winning De Kersentuin restaurant (see page 89).

Grand Hotel Krasnapolsky

Majestically presiding over a canal, the 17th-century Doelen Karena Hotel claims to have been visited by both Rembrandt and the Beatles

Dam 9 (tel: 55549111), 4-star, 323 rooms. Originally a truly elegant hotel, but now much of its air of class has been sacrificed for a modern look. Very central and handy for all shops and services.

throughout, yet placed in the old centre and handy for all services and shopping.

Jan Luyken Jan Luykenstraat 58 (tel: 5730730), 4-star, 63 rooms. Just across from the Leidseplein and handy for the Vondelpark and museums, a neat old-style place, some rooms with balconies.

Maas Leidsekade 91 (tel: 6233868), 3-star, plain but comfortable, 28 rooms. A bargain type hotel, facing a canal, not far from the centre and quietly situated.

Okura Amsterdam Ferdinand Bolstraat 333 (tel: 6787111), 5-star, 370 rooms. As its name implies, a Japanese hotel beyond the central district, on a canal.

Pulitzer Prinsengracht 315 (tel: 5235235), 5-star, 232 rooms. Quite simply a unique place – it consists of a group of canal houses cunningly converted to make a hotel of rare distinction. Every room is different and beautifully contrived. There are internal courts and gardens and art galleries too.

If you are going to town in Amsterdam, this is the place for you.

Ramada Renaissance Amsterdam Kattengat 1 (tel: 6212223), 5-star, 432 rooms. A strikingly modern hotel, which is well placed in a central location on canals and within easy reach of the main shopping streets, craft centre etc, surrounded by old canal houses.

Roemer Visscher Roemer Visscherstraat 10 (tel: 6125511), 3-star, very comfortable, 50 rooms. A usefully placed medium price hotel on a street

Holiday Inn Amsterdam De Boelelaan 2 (tel: 6462300), 5-star, 263 rooms. Near the Amstel, yet quite a way from the centre, this bold black block surmounted with the name in lights is a landmark. Handy for drivers.

Holiday Inn Crowne Plaza NZ Voorburgwal 5 (tel: 6200500), 5-star, 270 rooms. A classic Holiday Inn interior and modern

ACCOMMODATION

near the museums.
Swissôtel Amsterdam Ascot
Damrak 95-98 (tel: 6260066),
4-star, 109 rooms. A new
addition to the city's supply of
hotels, the Ascot is very
centrally placed near the Dam
and is well designed with views
from its front rooms in a
modern canal-house style
building.

Hostels

Hostels can be a good answer
for those on a budget. There are
several in Amsterdam run by
various bodies but best known
are the Dutch youth hostel
association, the Stichting
Nederlandse Jeugdherberg
Centrale (NJHC), Prof Tulpplein
4, 1018 GX Amsterdam (tel:
5513155). There are two hostels
in Amsterdam itself:
Stadsdoelen,
Kloveniersburgwal 97 (tel:
6246832). Open spring to
autumn.
Vondelpark, Zandpad 5 (tel:
6831744).
They are not restricted to the
young alone, and families and
older people are welcomed
provided they hold membership
in their own country, or have an
international youth hostel card.
Rates are very low, with prices
varying according to the
category of accommodation.
Cooking facilities are available
in some hostels (there are about
40 youth hostels in Holland). The
NJHC also concerns itself with
group accommodation. Very
cheap, the **Sleep-in
Maurikskade**, 's
Gravesandestraat 51, is useful.
Information and a bar too (tel:
6947444).

Bed and Breakfast

Family atmosphere and the
chance to meet the Amsterdam
people are the attractions of a
stay in a Dutch private house.
You may find difficulty in
locating these places which are
basically bed-and-breakfast
establishments, but do also
provide an evening meal as a
rule.
For further information and
reservations contact Bed and
Breakfast in Holland,
Warmondstraat 129 le, 1058
KV Amsterdam (tel: 020-
6157527).
You will need to book in
advance as this type of
accommodation is limited,
especially in summer.

Self-catering

Self-catering houses and
cottages on the outskirts of the
city (and also some flats right in
town) can be found for people
who do not wish to stay in
hotels. The tourist office should
have details of such rentals,
and cottage accommodation
can also be booked through the
NRC (see page 95), but again
for summer booking you will
need to make reservations as
early as possible. A group can
often find very favourable rates
in rented accommodation, and
if you choose carefully you can
find places that are close to
bus and tram connections into
the city.

Camping

Camping is allowed only on
specific sites in Holland. You
cannot spend the night in a
camper or caravan in a parking
lot or lay-by.

ENTERTAINMENT AND NIGHTLIFE

There are scores of theatres in Amsterdam, most small and presenting anything from dance and mime to modern Dutch plays. There are occasional plays in English to be seen but most popular with foreigners are the ballet, the opera and the concerts of classical music. A new theatre is a landmark in Amsterdam now, the Muziektheater which opened its doors in 1986 and became the home of the Netherlands Opera and the National Ballet. These important companies give

The Rembrandtplein is where it all happens at night. The square is lined with lively bars, clubs and restaurants

seasons, but the visitor might also try some of the small, almost pocket-size theatres that can be found all over Amsterdam. There is plenty of music to be heard in the city, and many visiting attractions. The centre for the thriving entertainment industry of Amsterdam is the Leidseplein which, as well as the massive Stadsschouwburg, is a centre for street entertainers.

Theatres/Concert Halls

Beurs van Berlage, Damrak. The Netherlands Philharmonic Orchestra perform in the old stock exchange building.
Concertgebouw, Concertgebouwplein. This is Holland's most famous concert hall, and presents an enormous number of concerts over the

ENTERTAINMENT AND NIGHTLIFE

year, often with star instrumentalists and conductors. It is renowned for its fine acoustics. An impressive place with its bold 19th-century design, it is the home of the Concertgebouw Orchestra, the major Dutch classical orchestra. Not all concerts are expensive however: there is a series of free lunchtime concerts, usually Wednesdays at 12.30.

Melkweg, off Leidseplein. This is more of a centre for alternative culture than just a theatre – there are many attractions housed under the 'Milky Way's' one roof. Here you will find pop concerts, 'happenings', alternative theatre, exhibitions and a café. Entry is normally by membership, but you can usually enter by day at the café entrance on the Marnixstraat. At night the scent of marijuana is often wafted on the air.

Muziektheater, Waterlooplein. A striking development beside the Stadhuis (City Hall) on the Amstel, this ought to be visited if only just to stroll through its

*The Stadsschouwburg theatre
houses the Dutch Public Theatre. It
was formerly the home of the
national opera and ballet
companies*

companies and there are also
seasons by leading
international companies, mostly
opera and ballet. The nearby
Waterlooplein has a handy
Metro station and the centre is
well served with trams and bus
services – there is a large car
park under the Muziektheater.
Stadsschouwburg, Leidseplein.
This big old-style theatre
dominates one side of the
square and its arcade is a home
for all sorts of alternative
entertainers. Plays, some opera
and ballets are presented in the
auditorium with its proscenium
arch stage, making a stately
setting for a special evening.
Many international companies
are presented here, but plays
are usually in Dutch. The
arcade in front of the theatre is
popular with street entertainers
who make this foot passage
their headquarters.

Dance
There are good dance
companies in Amsterdam, both
big and small, and the major
ones have a high standing
around the world, with a
particular style fostered by
native dancers and
choreographers of very high
calibre. You *can* see
productions of the classical
works, but most likely events
are modern works of stark
beauty, stressing the physicality
and sheer ability of the human
body to move in compelling
ways. Dutch dance style can be
surprising and innovative.
The National Ballet is a major
company which gives regular
seasons at the Muziektheater,
its home base. This company

foyers (when there is no
performance in progress). The
main theatre is semi-circular
and seats 1,600. But the
Muziektheater is more than just
a theatre, it is a parade of
places – restaurants, cafés,
shops and a booking office for
all events. It is home to the
national ballet and opera

ENTERTAINMENT AND NIGHTLIFE

presents both classical and modern ballet, while the Netherlands Dance Theater, which occupies a new theatre in the seat of government at The Hague, can be seen in works stressing contemporary origins and almost always originating within the company, although some works from abroad are incorporated in the repertoires of both groups. Both companies are top class and well worth getting to know. For the activities of small companies and individual dancers in Amsterdam, check entertainment listings or look for posters around the town, especially in the university area, or in the arcade in front of the Stadsschouwburg.

Opera
The other resident company of the Muziektheater is the Netherlands Opera which shares the space and seasons with the ballet. Besides productions of major operatic works you can see experimental works, and these are often presented during the period of the Holland Festival, an annual event in June, which is a very good time for the arts lover to visit the city. The Netherlands Opera is a major company with full chorus and a complete orchestra, usually the Nederlands Philharmonisch, and sometimes there are guest stars.

Tickets
Tickets can be bought at the theatre itself (Monday to Saturday from 10.00, Sundays from 12.00), from the VVV office

at Stationsplein, or from the AUB (Amsterdam Uit Buro) which sell tickets for all major events from its office on the Leidseplein/corner of Marnixstraat (Monday to Saturday 10.00 to 18.00). Book tickets from abroad from the Netherlands Reservation Centre (see page 95).

Nightclubs, Bars and Cafés
There are many nightclubs and cafés where you can hear music, or individual singers. African music is popular, so also is jazz both classical and funk, and the clubs around the Rembrandtplein are the places to find it. Most of these spots are open every night, some are weekends only, but the

ENTERTAINMENT AND NIGHTLIFE

Live music continues until the early hours in many of the city's bars, cafés and nightclubs

programmes usually start late and go on well into the small hours.

A walk along the Reguliersdwarsstraat will give you a sample of Amsterdam's nightlife. Cafés and bars usually stay open until 01.00 during the week and later at weekends, but nightclubs and cabarets will continue well into the small hours. The style is intimate, small and crowded and the variety on offer is very wide from the newest experiments in punk to old-style Latin music. Even neighbourhood bars will have a piano, whether a 'brown bar' or the newer style 'white bars' often done up in modern interpretations of Art Deco. These are popular with a younger crowd and so are the multi-media spots, noisy and brash yet good for finding out what's new. Amsterdam must be unusual in that its bars and clubs are friendly, there's little sense of the shady or underhand (if you discount the use of soft-drugs, which can seem unusual to the non-Hollander), and you are not likely to get ripped off or stuck with huge bills at the end of an evening.

Amsterdam also has clubs for gay men (notably at the Kerkstraat and along the Warmoesstraat close by the

ENTERTAINMENT AND NIGHTLIFE

Dam, and on the Reguliersdwarsstraat near the Muntplein) and also for lesbians. Information on meeting places and cafés is available from a useful central office and café at Rozenstraat 8 called the COC, open Wednesdays to Sundays until 18.00. There are discos for the local community here and for visitors every Friday, Saturday and Sunday night until late (tel: 6231192).

Bars
Almost all the principal hotels in the city will have bars (and they will be open most of the time) but for more atmosphere try the following:
Bamboo Bar, Lange Leidsedwarstraat, for blues and jazz
Bourbon Street Jazz and Blues Club, Leidsekruisstraat 6-8,

Liberated life in Amsterdam: women dance the night away in one of several gay bars to be found in the city

'bluesy jazz'
Café Alto, Korte Leidsedwarstraat 115, traditional jazz
Ciel Bleu, Hotel Okura, Ferdinand Bolstraat 333, piano bar
Clock Bar, Holiday Inn, de Boelelaan 2, piano bar
Costes, Rosmarijnsteeg 9, Oriental jazz from Japan
De IJsbreker, Weesperzijde 23, very much a local Dutch place with unusual new music
Joseph Lam Jazzclub, van Diemenstraat 242, for Dixieland
Odeon Kelder, Singel 460, disco with late night concerts
The String, Nes 98, folk and blues music

Cafés and Brown Bars
Café Américain, Leidseplein 28 in the American Hotel
Café Gollem, Raamsteeg 4
Hoppe, Spui 18-20
Café Kolkhaven, Prinsengracht 283, very old well preserved bar and café
Melkweg, Lijnbaansgracht 234a, media café popular with the young
O'Henry's, Rokin 89, an attempt at a British pub
Papeneiland, Prinsengracht 2, famous old brown café
De Smoeshaan, Leidsekade 90
De Zeilvaart, de Ruyterkade 106
Also try De Saloon, Eijders, Het Café.

Dancing
Boston Club in the Ramada Renaissance Hotel, Kattengat 1
Juliana's in the Hilton Hotel, Apollolaan 138-140
Lido, Max Euweplein 64
Mazzo, Rozengracht 114

Tulips herald the start of Holland's tourist season

WEATHER AND WHEN TO GO

Amsterdam has mild winters, and cool summers; the driest time is from February to May. See the chart, page 107. Amsterdam will forever be associated with tulips and bulbs of every type, and of course the months of April and May bring in many visitors to see Holland's bulbfields. At any time of the year, however, Amsterdam is an ideal place to go to for a break.

SPECIAL EVENTS
February
● International fashion fair (MODAM) at the Rai.
● A carnival takes place each year (end of month/early March) with a large parade through the centre

SPECIAL EVENTS

March
- Rowing events on the River Amstel.
- Heineken Tournament
- Boat Show, Rai
- Spring flower show at the Artis Zoo (for exact dates ask at the VVV Tourist Office in Holland or, from abroad, check with Netherlands Board of Tourism)
- The lighting of various important and interesting architectural features of the city starts, best viewed from the water

April
- The birthday of the Queen on 30 April is celebrated with many events

May
- Concert of ships' horns, bells and whistles on the IJ-harbour

June
- The Vondel Park has a series of open-air performances (until August)
- The International Royal Holland Cup is rowed
- The annual Holland Festival takes place for the entire month and occupies a number of places around the city (early reservation for major events is necessary)

July
- Carillon concerts from the main churches in July and August
- Summer festival of the smaller theatres

August
- International fashion fair (MODAM) at the Rai

September
- Jordaan district has its own folk festival
- Car rally (Dutch Championship)

- City marathon
- The huge flower market at Aalsmeer (see pages 33-4), in the suburbs of Amsterdam, is the focus of an annual flower parade, the Bloemencorso

October
- The major autumn flower show, the Herfsttentoonstelling, at the Bosmuseum

November
- A Stage Door Festival

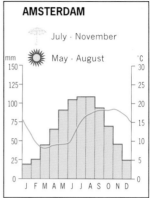

Windmills are now comparatively few and far between since electric power has taken over for pumping out the canals

• International horse show
The big Christmas show in the city is that of Sint Nicholaas who presides over a lavish parade in mid-November finishing on the Prins Hendrikkade, appropriately at the St Nicolaas Kerk, the principal Roman Catholic church of Amsterdam. The main figure of the procession is Sint Nicholaas himself, an elderly and benign gent who is the Dutch equivalent of Santa Claus. With flowing white hair and beard, he rides a white horse along the major roads of the city accompanied by retainers in costume; the venerable saint wears the robes and mitre of a bishop and carries a gilded crozier. Children come in hordes to line the streets.

Also of note:
• There is an Easter opening of the state rooms of the Royal Palace, and a summer opening for the months of June, July and August
• The market on the Nieuwmarkt, with all sort of objects both old and not-so-old, is open from mid-May until the end of September, 10.00 to 16.00
• Every Sunday on the Thorbeckeplein there is an open

air art market, from April to November

● The Rijksmuseum is the place for special art exhibitions throughout the year.

HOW TO BE A LOCAL

Although Amsterdam is a crowded city the residents enjoy life, and the spirit is infectious.

● To feel like a local try the 'brown bars' which are everywhere, for old-style drinking and socialising.

● For a younger and livelier set (and probably less of the pipe and tobacco smoke that turned them brown to begin with!) try the newer versions, or the fashionable white cafés, to be found mostly in the central and smarter districts. To feel really one of the crowd, try the famed *jenever* gin – drunk neat.

● Teashops are scattered all over the city and are almost always busy. The coffee room at the American Hotel is a local institution, with newspapers on long poles.

● The Dutch are usually affable and outgoing. They seem to enjoy meeting British people (older ones still cherish friendships made with the liberating army after World War II) and are helpful and hospitable. You should find it easy to strike up a conversation. By and large, the Dutch are free-thinking and liberal, so topics of conversation can be varied. The only problem is that they will quickly switch to English when they talk to you, even if you have mastered some Dutch phrases. It is not easy to practise Dutch in Amsterdam!

● To be really local, hire a bike. There are well-marked cycle paths in the suburbs and countryside. Try taking a picnic and sharing one of the permanent park barbecues. The Dutch congregate in parks and open spaces in the summer for concerts and other events, often taking picnics or drinks.

● Take rugs, sit on the grass, and enjoy the surroundings. The Vondel Park, with its woods, sports areas and lawns is very pleasant on summer evenings. Try the theatre, where the audiences will be mostly Dutch.

● There are many English-speaking theatres and performances of ballet, mime and opera have no language barriers (for ticket information see page 102). Try also the new Muziektheater. Locals enjoy promenading and sitting over coffee here, and you will get a great view of the Amstel.

● The Dutch are proud of their museums and Sundays will find crowds of them at the Rijksmuseum and others around the town. The same thing goes for the Artis Zoo, which is very popular with young families.

● The flea markets, such as the Waterlooplein (daily, except Sundays), draw big crowds. Try quick-food outlets – the quality of smoked or soused fish, sandwiches and warm doughnuts is usually good, and Dutch beer is excellent.

● Similarly, try shopping with the locals and explore street markets – these are places where there are produce and low-priced goods of all kinds. You won't see many tourists

Exploring the canals by pedalo

along the Haarlemmerstraat in the Jordaan district, or at the crowded Albert Cuyp market.

● Finally, consider staying with a Dutch family for bed and breakfast (see page 98).

CHILDREN

There is a great deal for children to do in the city and its environs. Teenagers will enjoy visits to places such as the Melkweg (see page 100) or the pop concerts in Vondel Park, or the many special events set up for younger visitors to museums and galleries (usually posted on gallery notice boards, or ask the VVV Tourist Office for any special events that are current). And remember that cycling is universal in Holland and both in the city and the country the special bike paths (separate from the main road and marked with a blue circle with a cyclist superimposed on it) are safe, if somewhat crowded at the rush hour. (See **Bicycles**, pages 115-16, for addresses of rental firms in Amsterdam). Older children will enjoy exploring the canals on their own in a pedalo for two or four (there are several rental points, see **Canal Boats**, pages 116-19) and they will be quite safe since the little craft are not

CHILDREN

Street Organs

Children will enjoy the big, brightly painted street organs that can be found at major central points. These large, unwieldy piped affairs in exotic and even lurid colours, run either by a belt or manually, hammer out Dutch tunes on crowded streets and squares, adding considerably to the atmosphere. One family maintains a tradition that is in danger of dying out, for the organs once common in all European cities, are becoming rare. Holland is now the only country where they can still be seen fairly frequently. There are estimated to be about 60 of them in the country, several having pitches in the centre of Amsterdam.

Amsterdam has over 40 musical and theatrical performances a day and among them there is bound to be something specially for children.

Simple pastimes such as riding the trams or finding the unusual among the many sculptures of Amsterdam can give much pleasure and children will of course find something of interest in many of the museums listed under **What to See**, pages 21-32. Worth mentioning in particular is the **Anne Frank Huis** where children can see attic room in which the teenage Anne and her family hid from the Germans during World War

Large, loud and luridly coloured street organs hammer out traditional Dutch tunes on busy squares and streets

flimsy and most canals are shallow.

Small organs and instruments are played by street musicians, while in summer the big churches usually have organ concerts which can be fascinating, for the organs are ancient instruments – the one in the Nieuwe Kerk beside the Dam dates from 1665, that of the Oude Kerk from 1724. There are 42 historic organs in the churches of the city. An interesting game can be played listening to carillons from the church towers – there are nine carillons in all – comparing and sometimes deciding exactly what time they are calling out. There are guided tours in churches and often a chance to climb the tower – fun for those whose legs are young! Note that

II and where she wrote her famous diary. See page 25-6 for details.

There is always the branch of **Madame Tussaud** to visit. The Madame Tussaud Scenerama features waxwork models of personalities from the 17th century to the present. Especially popular with children is a television studio complete with pop stars. Located at Dam 20; open daily 10.00 to 17.30; closed 30 April and 25 December.

Amsterdam has its own Children's Museum with a difference – the Kindermuseum. Adults may only go when accompanied by a child! There are lots of possibilities for learning, touching and doing here, and new exhibitions are regularly mounted. The

museum is especially meant for ages 6 to 12, but there is something for everyone.

There are permanent shows at the neighbouring **Tropenmuseum**, which is a museum of people of the tropics and sub-tropics. Innovative and architecturally exciting, a wide central court has the gallery floors opening on to it with an open, airy effect. Here, cunningly devised, are an Indian village, African market, North African street and a Javanese house. It is an intriguing place for anyone, but children will find lots to do here and there are special programmes on Saturday. Both museums are at Linnaeusstraat 2, near Mauritskade.

Another place loved by children, outside Amsterdam but well worth a day's outing, is **Madurodam**, in The Hague. This collection of miniature houses set in squares and streets which can be inspected at close quarters is world-famous and very popular and features all the major monuments of the country reproduced to scale – very much a children's scale. Detail is microscopic and children will love finding out the tiny aspects of the buildings, ranging from church towers to windmills. Open daily 09.00 to 22.30 (April to May), 23.00 (June to August), 21.30 (September) or 18.00 (October to December). Closed January to March.

You can combine a visit here (there are coach trips from the cities) with a discovery of **The Hague**, a compact city with lots to see in this centre of government (see **Excursions**

from Amsterdam, page 61–2).
Christmas Celebrations The great day for Amsterdam's children falls usually in mid-November when the much-loved Sint Nicholaas arrives by boat in the port of Amsterdam. The Bishop mounts a horse and tours the city, accompanied by his retainers known as the Black Peters, and families all turn out with the children to watch them pass. The costumed assistants throw gingernuts to the children, and there is huge excitement. On 5 December Eve (ie 4 December) families gather to give presents and poems to each other, and to mark the day of the patron saint of Amsterdam, and of sailors, good old St Nick, or of course, 'Sinterklaas', or the delightful old fellow known in so many different guises around the Christian world.

TIGHT BUDGET

● **Accommodation** There are plenty of youth hostels and low-price hotels. You can also camp on the outskirts of the city.

Merry-go-rounds are perennial favourites

Information from any VVV.
● **Cycling** Hire a bike – it's the cheapest way to get around.
● **Discounts** Ask about the **Holland Leisure Card**, available from Dutch tourist offices. It lasts one year and gives discounts on transport and other services – the **Holland Leisure Card Plus** allows free access to more than 350 museums.
● **Museum reductions** The Museumjaarkaart (annual museum ticket) gives free access to many of Amsterdam's museums and others in Holland for a year. Available from participating museums or the VVV.
● **Eating** There are lots of low-price cafeterias and pizza places, plus good quality, cheap wholefood restaurants. 'Tourist Menu' and 'Neerlands Dis' signs (see page 85). Try eating at markets. Some bars sell low-price drinks early in the evening.
● **Free Entertainment** There is lots around the Leidseplein, beside the Muziektheater and in the Vondel Park.
● **Public Transport** The cheapest tickets are strip tickets (*stripenkaarten*). Based on a zone system, they last one hour.
● **Local Markets** Fun, with plenty of bargains.
● **Student Reductions** For these you need an International Student Identity Card, or an International Young Person's Passport (see page 124).
● **Winter Visits** 'Winter, the Amsterdam Way' is a money-saving package operated by the Netherlands Board of Tourism (see pages 93–4).

DIRECTORY

Arriving

The Netherlands' main international airport is Schiphol, Amsterdam. Several companies run regular car and passenger ferries between Holland and the UK. Many travel companies do package trips to Amsterdam – Time Off and Travelscene among others. You will need a valid passport (no visa unless staying longer than three months) and a stay of longer than eight days in one place must be reported to the police (this formality, however, is covered by hotel registration).

Rail/Bus Connection KLM run a bus service from the airport to hotels in Amsterdam every half hour from 06.30 to 15.00, last departure 17.00. Better, however, is the train connection between Schiphol and the centre. Trains run about every 15 minutes (hourly through the night) and are part of the commuter service so not just bound for the airport. You'll need to check the departure boards and look for trains marked with a small aircraft

There's many a window like this, with its typical display of porcelain and flowers

Bulbs, bulbs and more bulbs!

besides 'Schiphol'. It will take you around 20 minutes. You may find luggage space is limited and there will be crowds at the rush hours.

Camping
Local campsites exist near the main Dutch cities and are well equipped and clean with all facilities. The VVV Tourist Office publishes a list of campsites in north Holland. The only document you will need is your passport. The fee for camping with tent or motorhome is low. The sites in Holland are well run and in addition there are also low price camp-type hostels.

Car Breakdown
Main highways have frequent patrols by police cars and the Royal Dutch Touring Club (ANWB) provides a nationwide 24-hour breakdown service to AIT-affiliated motoring club members. Telephone 06 0888 for assistance, or use the roadside emergency telephones on major highways.

Car Rental
Car rental is simple, with all the big agencies represented plus local ones, but, unless you are planning explorations beyond the city, with Amsterdam's chronic parking difficulties a car can just be a nuisance. Rental offices can be found at the airport and in central Amsterdam. You will need your national driving licence, and for some companies must be at least 21.

Chauffeur-driven Cars
Chauffeur-driven cars are available through the VVV Tourist Office, with guided tours if required, and airport pickups.

Chemists (see Pharmacies)

Crime
Crime is a problem in the city, since there is a good deal of drug trafficking. Take the usual precautions and do not walk in empty, dark alleys or leave items on car seats where they can be spotted and the car broken into. Women should wear their handbags across their bodies and men keep their wallets in upper pockets.

Customs Regulations
The normal EC regulations apply. Ordinary travellers will be unlikely to exceed the new, more generous EC duty-paid allowances, check with the Netherlands Board of Tourism. No meat, plants or weapons (including knives) may be imported.

City of canals and cycles: there are bicycles and bicycle parking racks everywhere – and plenty of rental agencies

Disabled Travellers

The Netherlands is a world leader in providing facilities for handicapped people.

Domestic Travel

Buses

Well served with frequent services all over the city on a flat fare basis (see **Transit Authority/GVB**, page 120).

Bicycles

If you are young and energetic then try joining in with the hordes of Amsterdammers who regularly cycle round the city. It is a great way for feeling you are a part of the city as you triumphantly get ahead of stalled traffic on the narrow streets or take a short cut. There are many bike rental agencies and the cost is low but you will need to put down a deposit. This is due to the high incidence of cycle theft in the city, so make sure the bike is secure when parked. You can even take a tour on a bike – *Ena's Bicycle Tour* which lasts seven and a half hours! (Information from VVV Tourist Office).

Rentals from:
Holland Rent-a-Bike, Damrak 247 (tel: 6223207). Big and popular.
Koenders Take-a-Bike,

DIRECTORY

Stationsplein 33 (tel: 6248391), low rates.
MacBike, Nieuwe Uilenburgerstraat 116 (tel: 6200985). Small and friendly, guided tours. Bicycles are parked all over the city – racks are everywhere – and the rush hour is a whizz on wheels. With so many bikes there are many pavement repair shops – the machines get a bumping with so many cobbled streets to negotiate. You can also rent mopeds reasonably. Outside the city there are cycle-only routes netting the entire country, the special paths marked with blue-and-white circular markers.

Paths for cyclists A round sign of a white cycle on a blue background indicates paths obligatory for cycles and mopeds. Optional paths are marked with small black signs saying 'fietspad' or 'rijwielpad' and are for cycles but not mopeds. Cycle lanes on main roads are marked with a white cycle on the road surface.

Canal Boats

You can take a water-bus trip, and these are very popular for giving you a feeling of the old aspects of Amsterdam from water level in big, comfortable boats leaving from various points, especially along Damrak and the Rokin. Check the advertising boards for prices and what you get. The boats will usually take you along the 'residential' canals under many low bridges and also give glimpses of the open waters of the IJsselmeer and the docks beyond the Centraal Station.

Centraal Station and Stationsplein – a busy place, with the main information centres

This is a novel and fascinating way to see the city. (Dinner cruises tend to be expensive and not a bargain.) The VVV Tourist Office at the main station has detailed schedules and prices of boat trips.
Canal boat companies (*rederijen*) and departure points:
Rederij d'Amstel, opposite Heineken Brewery (tel:

6265636)
Rederij Holland International,
opposite Centraal Station (tel
6227788)
Rederij P Kooij, Rokin, opposite
number 125 (tel: 6233810)
Rederij Lovers BV, Prins
Hendrikkade, opposite number
76 (tel: 6222181)
Meyers Rondvaarten, Damrak,
jetties 4 and 5 (tel: 6234208)
Rederij Noord-Zuid,
Stadhouderskade 25, opposite
Parkhotel (tel: 6791370)
Rederij Plas, Damrak, jetties 1–3
(tel: 6245406)

Canal Bus Shuttle service
running at 20-minute intervals
on the canals between Centraal
Station and the Rijskmuseum,
with three stops en route.
Museum Boat Combines a
canal trip and museum visit. It
runs to various city museums;
after visiting one museum catch
the next boat to travel on to
another one. (See also page
22.)
Special boat tours Some boats
will make special tours to
include pub visits, a tour of a
diamond factory, even a theatre

visit, but in general these are better arranged separately for yourself. Though it is true to say that in central Amsterdam you are never more than a few yards from a waterway. There is a useful publication obtainable from tourist offices in Holland and abroad called *Cruises in Amsterdam* that gives detailed information and times and charges. Some cruises are 90 minutes, some as long as two hours. Most boats operate from April until the end of October; during this time the canals are illuminated each night, while in the winter they are lit up two or three times a week. Church spires, house-fronts, bridges glow with lights giving a different and romantic aspect that negates the somewhat banal explanations given by the guide, or in some cases, the tape.

Canal boating on your own If you want to be adventurous then try a canal boat tour on your own – it is quite possible and consists of renting a pedal boat for two or four persons. It is a good way of seeing the little backwaters where the big boats don't ply. Expect to pay a deposit. *Canal Bike* has four moorings, so you can go from one and leave the pedal-boat at another; *Roëll* has three, the main one near the Amstel Inter Continental Hotel. Spring to autumn only, and the little rectangular craft are solid and safe.

The Damrak, leading into the Dam, at the heart of the city

Roëll: Mauritskade 1 (tel: 6929124)
Canal Bike: Amstel 57 (tel: 6265574)
Most companies will of course do group rentals for large boats, and also offer motorboats and 'family' boats. The large cruise boats have lavatories on board.

Cars
Drivers bringing in a car or other vehicle must produce a full driving licence, registration and road safety test certificate, proof of insurance in EC countries (a 'green card', or temporary insurance cover obtained at the border crossing), also an international identity disc affixed to the rear. Trailers and caravans must be 'used' or else a registration

certificate produced.
Speed Limits A general speed limit in built up areas of 50km per hour (31mph); in residential areas marked with a white house on a blue background cars should be driven at a walking pace. General speed limit outside built up areas, 80km per hour (49mph). On highways and motorways, 120km per hour (74mph).

Coach Tours
A number of special tours are available in Amsterdam giving you a good but rather isolated introduction to a city that really needs closer contact than the wide windows of a tourist bus. See the VVV for information on all kinds of tours not only of Amsterdam but of its nearby villages and other Dutch towns for half or full day explorations at reasonable rates, some with meals and token drinks included. The commentary is usually by a professional guide, but tapes are also used.

Metro/Light Railway
A new service of two major lines, which is often being extended, and will no doubt have more lines added. It serves central Amsterdam and works on the same fare basis as the trams and the buses, but is usually of little use to the tourist since it principally serves commuters coming in from the suburbs.

Trains
Centraal Station is of course a busy place with over 1,000 trains arriving and departing from the suburbs and principal

DIRECTORY

European centres. It is a useful place for departures to other locations around Amsterdam (see **Excursions from Amsterdam** pages 55-62). There is an information desk within the station providing all necessary facts about local travel.

Trams

There are 16 city lines and the big, wide trams can be seen all over the city. Bus and tram shelters have maps of the system encompassing the whole city, but unless you have friends or relations in the suburbs it is unlikely that you will need to go far afield.

Transit Authority/GVB

Centraal Station is a place you will not be able to avoid! It is surrounded by many useful services, a web of tramlines, and numerous stops that have all been updated to give

Kalverstraat, one of several central streets for pedestrians only

electronic information. Opposite the station is the office of the Amsterdam Transit Authority, or GVB. The GVB can supply you with all the information and requirements for getting about Amsterdam on public transport. It controls all bus and tram services, the two Metro lines, light railway and ferries. Pick up a map, information folder and as many free leaflets as you need.

Buying a ticket There are several kinds of tickets – you can use the basic single flat fare ticket purchased from the bus or tram driver, or you can get a day ticket from the bus or tram driver, or at Metro stations; tickets for between two and nine days are available only from the GVB. Strip tickets (*stripenkaarten*) are cheapest but need some understanding since they are based on a zone system and you will need to know how many zones you will cross before stamping them in the machine – always stamp one strip more than the number of zones you will cross. The city has 11 zones, but for many tourists the main central zone is all that is needed. The strip tickets are available in units of 2, 3 or 10, or sometimes 15, from the GVB, VVV, post offices newsagents and tobacconists. Once stamped, they are valid for an hour's travel and include transfers to other lines, the light railway and the Metro. Inspectors can fine you on the spot if you do not hold a valid time-stamped ticket **Times of services** Most of the bus and tram services start early in the morning and so does the Metro. They will go on until midnight, or after, when a night bus service begins (the GVB will also provide you with a *Night Buses* brochure). You can either pay the flat fare, or use a period ticket.

Taxis

Taxis carry a lighted sign on the roof when free and are hired as a rule from a taxi stand. (They do not always respond to being hailed.) They are metered except for journeys beyond the central area and into the country. (Schiphol counts as out of town and the fare will be around 50 guilders.) Tips are included in the metered fare, but are topped up by rounding the charge to the next guilder as a rule. Central taxi telephone number: 6777777.

Touristram

Operated by the VVV (see below), this service runs regularly. Most cities have special bus services for tourists, but Amsterdam operates one of her famous trams. For details and fares (it can be linked with Museumboat trip) check at the VVV Tourist Office.

Walking

This is the best way to see Amsterdam, and of course the cheapest, with shoe leather being your only concern. So pack a comfortable pair of shoes and also a warm casual outfit with a scarf and a folding umbrella (rain is common in Holland most of the autumn and winter) and set off. You do not have to have a map but it is handy and by day you can go almost anywhere safely. (Two suggested routes are included in this book, on pages 46-55.) You will find that several central streets are for walkers only, notably the central shopping streets of Kalverstraat and Nieuwendijk which snake through the middle of the city. Do not make the mistake of confusing cycle paths with footpaths in some of the more recently developed areas because the two-wheelers, often with an extra passenger on the back, can hurtle along at high speed and at night lights are a rarity, so you do not always see cyclists coming! Walks planned with care can always end at a bus or tram stop and you can ride back home. You are not likely to get lost either, because the U-shaped plan of central

No excuse needed to stop off for an ice cream – like all Dutch dairy products, it is creamy and delicious

Amsterdam means that in quick time you will cross a canal and find where you are, and the streets, despite often long and unwieldy names almost impossible to pronounce for the non-Dutch speaker, are well marked on the corners with neat blue and white markers. In addition a new sign has been appearing on Amsterdam's streets, a series of pointers attached to lamp-posts and showing clearly on their orange and grey rectangular shapes the directions of tourist attractions. There are guided tours of the city on offer, walking with a group leader who is usually a registered guide.

Like any city, Amsterdam constantly changes, so check for latest information on new routes at the VVV.

Electricity
220 volts. Two round-pin plugs.

Embassies and Consulates
Great Britain: Koningslaan 44 (tel: 6764343) (Consulate)
USA: Museumplein 19 (tel: 6790321) (Consulate)
Diplomatic representation for Australia and Canada is in The Hague.

Emergency Telephone Numbers
National
Police, fire, ambulance: 06-11
Amsterdam
Police: 6222222
Ambulance: 5555555
Doctor/dentist: 6642111
SOS Dentist: 6791821
Tourist assistance: 6239314

Entertainment Information
The best source of information is the fortnightly English-language magazine, *What's on in Amsterdam*, available from the VVV or newsstands.

Health
Foreign visitors have the right to medical assistance in accordance with the Dutch health service law. Those originating from within EC countries will need an insurance form which can be obtained before leaving home – in the UK ask at the post office for leaflet T4, containing form E111. If you need medical help in Amsterdam you must

produce the completed E111 to receive free treatment, but any prescribed medicines must be paid for. Private medical insurance is always a good idea.

Lost Property
Waterlooplein 11 (tel: 65598005)
Open: Monday to Friday 11.00 to 15.30
Tram, bus and metro: Prins Hendrikkade 108-114 (tel: 5514911) *Open*: Monday to Friday 08.30 to 15.30. **Trains:** Centraal Station (tel: 5578544) *Open*: daily 07.00 to 22.00.

Money Matters
There are no import and export restrictions on local or foreign currencies. Money can be changed at the official GWK offices at airports, stations and at border points. Besides cash you can also change traveller's cheques, and credit card transactions for cash. Money can also be exchanged at banks and at post offices and at certain VVV Tourist Offices. Commissions can vary widely, so look around at the various possibilities especially if exchanging large sums.
The money system is based on the guilder (NLG); you may also see abbreviations f, fl, Hfl, Dfl. There are a hundred cents to the guilder, though the smallest coin is now a five cent piece. Credit cards are accepted everywhere in Amsterdam for sales in restaurants, hotels, shops, and at stations for tickets for trains or at airports for air tickets. Car rental agencies also accept leading credit cards,

and the main ones (American Express, Diners Club, Eurocard and Visa) all have principal offices in the country.

Opening Times

Banks
Open Monday to Friday 09.00 to 16.00/17.00 and sometimes later on Thursday and Friday late-night shopping evenings. (GWK at Schipol Station and Centraal Station are open 24 hours.)

Shops
Monday to Friday 08.30/09.00 to 17.30/18.00; Saturdays shops close 16.00/17.00. Shops have individual closing days or half days, indicated by signs. Late-night shopping on Thursdays or Fridays.

Museums
Main museums from 10.00 to 17.00;. Sunday from 13.00; closed Monday.

Post Offices (see page 124)

Pharmacies
For details of evening and Sunday opening contact the Central Doctors' Service (tel: 6642111).

Places of Worship
For foreign language services and times of local ones ask at the VVV Tourist Office.

Police
In Amsterdam the police have a special alarm number: 6222222 The main office is at Elandsgracht 117, (tel: 5599111)

DIRECTORY

Post Office

The Main Post Office on Singel 250-256 is open every weekday from 08.30 to 18.00 (Thursday until 20.00). Saturdays from 09.00 to 15.00. Closed Sundays. Letters can be received here and held for pick up (Poste Restante). Post boxes have two slots, one for local and one for abroad. To post parcels use the post office at the Oosterdokskade 5, open weekdays 08.30 to 21.00; Saturday 09.00 to 12.00.

Public Holidays

New Year's Day
Good Friday
Easter Sunday and Monday
Queen's Birthday (30 April)
Ascension Day
Whit Sunday and Monday
Christmas Day
Boxing Day

Student and Youth Travel

Students aged 16 to 30 may qualify for the International Young Person's Passport, giving discounts on museums, galleries, theatres, student hotels and restaurants. It is available from the NBBS travel agency, Leidsestraat 53, Amsterdam (tel: 6381736).

Telephone

International calls can be made from phone boxes or from post offices by dialling 09 and, when tone changes, the international code then the area code minus the initial 0. Calls from hotels are more expensive.

Time Difference

Central European Time Zone (so most of the year Amsterdam is one hour ahead of London, six hours ahead of New York).

Tipping

Almost always included in hotels and restaurant bills, you can add a little extra for good service if you wish. Taxi meters include a tip, although it is customary to round up fares to the nearest guilder.

Toilets

As always, easier for men than women but they are not plentiful in the city and the best way is to use hotels or cafés where you can usually find adequate and clean facilities (keep small coins in hand for tips for attendants).

Tourist Information

Netherlands Board of Tourism (NBT)

Australia: 5 Elizabeth Street, Sydney NSW 2000 (tel: 02 247 6921)
Canada: 25 Adelaide Street East, Toronto, Ontario M5C 1Y2 (tel: 416 363 1577)
UK: PO Box 523, London SW1E 5NT (tel: 0891 200277)
USA: 355 Lexington Avenue (21st floor), New York, NY 10017 (tel: 212 370 7360)

VVV Amsterdam Tourist Offices

Information is available from the Stationsplein office, open all year every day (tel: 34034066). For information in advance, write to PO Box 3901, 1001 AS Amsterdam, The Netherlands. There are also offices on the corner of Leidsestraat and Leidseplein, and the corner of Stadionplein and Van Tuyll van Serooskerkenweg.

LANGUAGE

yes ja
no nee
please alstublieft
thank you
dank u, or dank u wel
hello dag
**good morning/afternoon/
evening** goede morgen/
middag/avond
are you well?
hoe gaat het met u?
very well uitstekend
pardon me/excuse me
pardon
breakfast ontbijt
dinner diner
sandwich broodje
cup of coffee/tea
kopje koffie/thee
dish of the day dagschotel
may I order?
mag ik even bestellen?
how much does this cost?
wat kost dit?
may I pay?
mag ik even afrekenen?
**inclusive of VAT and service
charge** inclusief BTW en
bedieningsgeld
open open
closed gesloten
no entry verboden toegang
a ticket to... een kaartje naar...
one-way ticket enkele reis
return retour
where's the... waar is de...?
post office postkantoor
chemist apotheek
hospital ziekenhuis
doctor dokter
station station
bank bank
postcard briefkaart
letter box brievenbus
telephone booth telefooncel
one een
two twee

*The hungry tourist is spoiled for
choice with the wide range of
cuisine, at a wide range of prices*

three drie
four vier
five vijf
six zes
seven zeven
eight acht
nine negen
ten tien

To try to speak Dutch you will
need a dictionary and a
procunciation guide. There are
a few basic rules that may help
with pronunciation

ee is pronounced 'ay'
g on its own is a guttural sound
almost like an h
j is normally soft as in 'yah' for
ja (yes) or else not sounded at
all
oo is usually shorter than it
appears and makes the sound
'oh'.
IJ is pronounced 'eye'.

INDEX/ACKNOWLEDGEMENTS

ACKNOWLEDGEMENTS

The Automobile Association would like
to thank the following photographers
and libraries for their assistance in the
compilation of this book

INTERNATIONAL PHOTOBANK 8/9
waterbus & canal, 36 Montelbaanstoren,
42/3 Skinny Bridge, 115 bicycles.

NATURE PHOTOGRAPHERS LTD 63
black tailed godwit (T Andrewartha),
64/5 sea holly, 75 pool frog (P R Sterry),
67 yellow horned poppy (R Tidman),
68/9 Bewick swan, 70 Friesland (C & J
Knights), 72/3 bittern (J Wilson).

CHRISTINE OSBORNE PICTURES 7 eel
fishermen, 10/11 buildings, 13
transport, 23 van Gogh Museum, 24/5
Historisch Museum, 26/7 Joods
Historisch Museum, 30/1 Wheatfield,
van Gogh Museum, 33 Willet-
Holthuysen Museum, 34 Singel flower
market, 39 New Church, 40 Red Light
District, 44 clogs, 46/7 canal houses, 53
Westerkerk, 54 Alkmaar cheese
market, 56 Delft porcelain factory, 61
tulips, 77 Schiphol airport, 78/9 Dutch
cheeses, 80 antique shop, 82 flea
market, 83 shopping for diamonds, 85
smoked eels, 86/7 Indonesian food, 88
café society, 90/1 Indonesian restaurant,
93 accommodation, 94 The American
Hotel, 99 night lights, 100/1
Stadsschouwburg theatre, 102/3 café,
104 womens' gay bar, 105 tulips, 106/7
windmill, 109 pedalos on the canal, 112
merry-go-round, 113 window, 116/7
Centraal Station, 118/9 shops, 120
Kalvestraat, 122 ice cream, 125 menu.

SPECTRUM COLOUR LIBRARY Cover:
Keizersgracht, 14/5 doorway, 16/7
houses & café, 18 house front, 28
stained glass window, 51
Rembrandtplein, 96/7 Doelen Crest
Hotel, 100/1 street organ, 114 bulb
market.

ZEFA PICTURE LIBRARY (UK) LTD 4
Amsterdam, 21 Rijksmuseum.

Author's acknowledgements

The author is indebted to Marcel
Belthus at the Netherlands Board of
Tourism, and Travelscene for
assistance in the preparation of this
book.